Photo: Garth Lenz

13,127 board feet of framing lumber • 6,212 square feet of sheathing • 13.97 tons of concrete • 2,325 square feet of exterior siding material • 3,100 square feet of roofing material • 3,061 square feet of insulation • 6,144 square feet of interior wall material • 120 linear feet of ducting • 15 windows • 13 kitchen cabinets • 2 other cabinets • 1 kitchen sink • 12 interior doors • 7 closet doors • 2 exterior doors • 1 patio door • 2 garage doors • 1 fireplace • 3 toilets • 2 bathtubs • 1 shower stall • 3 bathroom sinks • 2,085 square feet of flooring material such as carpeting, resilient sheet, resilient tile, ceramic tile or wood plank • 1 range • 1 refrigerator • 1 dishwasher • 1 garbage disposal • 1 range hood • 1 washer • 1 dryer

Materials used in building a 2,085-square-foot single-family home. Source: National Association of Home Builders.

CONSTRUCTION WITHOUT DESTRUCTION

Randy Hayes

Can building with the right materials really help the world's environmental problems? Absolutely. By carefully choosing construction materials and building approaches, you can influence the fate of the world's forests and help orchestrate a U-turn toward an ecologically sustainable society.

From Alaska to Alabama, and from Asia to the Amazon, old-growth forests are still falling for U.S. home building. In the process, the extinction of countless glorious creatures and the loss of their important functions in the web of life are accelerating; deforestation is also contributing to the extreme weather events that are increasingly pounding our planet. Even the United Nations has warned of the potentially catastrophic and irreversible impacts of global warming. If we do not resolve our relationship to nature and our constructed world, history will be justifiably unkind to us. Conversely, a concerted effort could, in our lifetime, lead us away from the deforestation crisis and toward a healthier planet that supports all people and all creatures.

Can we still use wood? Yes, recycled materials as well as wood from trees outside of threatened forests, which have been cut under strict ecological logging criteria and certified by a credible, independent, third party. This certification approach must include a chain-of-custody that helps us follow the trail from the forest to the job site. Regardless of what building material is used, however, it is important to remember that virtually all production methods consume energy and water, require resource extraction, and generate pollution and waste of some sort. Whenever possible, we should do our best to reduce building material consumption and make the best possible use of those resources we do choose.

Recent trends give us reason for hope. Polling data suggest that a majority of Americans want to see old-growth forests protected. Since 1999, numerous home improvement retailers have committed to eliminating wood products from endangered forests, while simultaneously phasing in Forest Stewardship Council (FSC)-certified wood and other non-wood alternatives. Our organization is working with companies to help them implement bans on logging, sales, and use of old growth. It's now up to those companies still logging old growth in the United States to adapt to these changes in the marketplace, and shift from old-growth exploitation towards responsible forest stewardship.

Wild, naturally evolving forests are an essential component of the biosphere's life-support system. They are also home to many of the world's vast array of life forms. The deforestation crisis requires a surgical cut away from industrial society's increasing dependence on wood from natural forests. Over time, this approach will increase the quantity and quality of forest ecosystems and enhance the vital services they provide for all Earth's inhabitants.

To that end, the Rainforest Action Network has launched a six-fold plan to halt deforestation and its consequences. Our platform includes:

- Global forest protection, including an end to logging of ancient old-growth forests;
- Ecologically certified logging outside of ancient old-growth forests with strict criteria for maintenance of biological diversity;
- Diversified fiber supply (such as tree-free papers, and building and packaging materials), relying on 'waste' products wherever possible;
- Consumption reduction, especially in the over-developed nations;
- Transformation of government and corporate policy;
- Sustainable economic development based on working with nature, rather than against it.

Nature—with its complex, local, ecological systems and myriad life forms—cannot speak at our construction sites. The mahogany tree and black leopard have no voice in our government chambers, corporate boardrooms, or local wood shops. It is our responsibility to speak on their behalf as best we can. We cannot ask for too much. And we had better not ask for too little. There is still time to change paths and stabilize what remains of natural forests, while providing for society's construction needs. We must each aggressively do our part. You can take an important step today by studying the materials and building approaches featured in this book, and by contributing to a new vision, one of construction without excessive destruction, one project at a time.

Randy Hayes is the president of the San Francisco-based Rainforest Action Network. He can be contacted at www.ran.org.

BUILDING AS IF THE FORESTS MATTERED

Sim Van der Ryn

First, a confession. I designed and built my share of wood homes, some of them out of old-growth materials. Wood, in the form of dimensional lumber, is simply a wonderful material: easy to work with, warm to the eyes and hand, natural, reasonably durable, the material that defines the trade of carpentry and the standard material for houses and light buildings in North America.

But there are reasons I've looked for other ways to build. I was born in Holland, a country with almost no forests and lots of clay. There, as in most of Europe, masonry is the material of choice for light construction, and it is the building industry standard. Visiting the United States for the first time, my Italian son-in-law was incredulous at our profligate use of wood—a material he considered inferior to masonry in terms of durability, fire resistance and maintenance.

About thirty-five years ago, I started experimenting with alternatives to standard wood construction. My partner and I designed low-cost housing with an early panel system using 4x8 plywood sheets bonded to styrofoam cores. I built a weekend home for my family using this system for floors, walls, and roofs. Then I discovered recycled materials, which in the 1960s and 70s could often be had for nothing if you showed up at the right time with a flatbed truck at a demolition site. The house I live in now has windows from old East Bay trains, beams from a dismantled Mendocino mill, stairs made from recycled wine tanks—all free for the asking.

Ancient old-growth forests are the keystone species of unique and awe-inspiring ecosystems—the lungs of our planet, and the host to the greatest diversity of life—whose value to society far exceeds any monetary value to a forest owner. Cutting and using any newly cut old-growth woods—our forest relatives—is the moral equivalent of murdering our living grandparents. I built the exterior of my cottage walls out of salvaged old-growth straight grain Douglas fir that had already spent a useful life as the floors of chicken coops. Thirty years later, they show no wear. Why? Study the growth rings on trees that grew slowly. The densely packed cells in the rings of winter growth may be as many as twenty to the inch. Then examine most newly harvested second- and third-growth timber that has grown up rapidly. The summer sapwood growth between the dense winter rings now fills most of the space. In the weather, it oxidizes and rots quickly unless it is constantly painted, and even then it won't last more than several generations.

The non–old-growth wood available today is inferior to the old growth we used in the past. The answer is to use no new wood in the building shell exposed to the weather and in the building frame. Go to other materials and the manufactured wood products featured in this book. Use wood—reclaimed or new—very sparingly for indoor accents, for cabinetry, and special details that feature its warmth and beauty. Reduce the amount of newly harvested wood in homes by 50 to 80 percent and our children and grandchildren may get to experience forests that are more than the sylvan equivalent of cornfields.

Today, as this timely and useful book outlines, we seem to have a multitude of choices available to us in designing and building without destroying forests or polluting the planet. The building products industry—which spends less on research and development than any other industry—is beginning to change because of economic and environmental pressures. In fact, it's difficult for an innovative, environmentally conscious office such as ours to keep up with all the new products and evaluate the various claims made for many of them. For the homeowner or casual builder, the environmental building marketplace presents a dizzying array of choices and claims. It's an exciting time to be an environmental architect!

There are many economic and durable home shell construction systems that are preferable to wood. Our office has used many of these, including straw-bale, stabilized soils, recycled industrial and agricultural fiber and cement boards, steel, even photovoltaic cells that generate electricity while they protect you from the weather. Today, steel is our most recycled building material. A host of other industrial and agricultural waste products and plastics are all good candidates for recycling into new building components.

The total market share of all these products is still very small compared to the total light construction market, and the number of buildings that integrate multiple systems is smaller still. We are in the early stages of a green building revolution. Wider acceptance by consumers and builders will come about as issues and answers become clearer to builders and the general public.

Many people still associate green architecture with the crude experiments of the back-to-the-land 1970s. I plead guilty to designing and building my share of leaky greenhouses, slanting solar walls, clumsy solar hot water heaters, and a mine shaft aesthetic. People don't understand the potential for common sense integration of climate responsive design and materials such as wall and roof panels that produce electricity directly from the sun. Soon builders will be offering green showcase homes to their buyers that create a new, graceful and up-to-date natural aesthetic.

The toughest question is how to make decisions regarding design, materials, and systems when there seem to be so many choices. Interest in green materials and sustainable building techniques is growing rapidly among all types of clients—private, corporate, institutional. It is difficult even for professionals to sort out claims from reality. Lacking independent third party-verification—'The Green Seal'—it is difficult, often impossible, for lay people or even professionals to properly evaluate materials and systems from a sustainable perspective.

Many clients become overly involved in the details before concentrating on more basic design strategies that determine a building's true value, true cost, and its ultimate contribution to a more sustainable society. Some of these principles are listed at the end of Chapter One, "Basics of Resource Efficient Building" (see page 14). I would like to add the questions we ask of clients—the Five Points of Green Building underlying Van der Ryn Architects' and the Ecological Design Institute's approach to sustainable building.

Is it a Tough Building? A tough building is designed to last a long time by specifically addressing the different life cycles of its major component systems. British Architect Frank Duffy identifies five categories from typically longest to shortest life span as follows: site, structure, systems (mechanical, electrical etc.), skin, and 'stuff,' i.e. furniture and equipment. But with new materials, these life spans change, and thus the entire design may change. We have found, for example, that the systems for thick wall earth houses, where the skin has a very long life and is difficult to change, must be designed with redundant conduit and ducting for rapid technological change in communications and other systems. Another example is in the commercial building sector. The typical in-the-ceiling high-pressure ductwork is inefficient from an energy and user comfort point of view. Changing office layouts and wiring is cumbersome and time-consuming. This has led to the growing use of low-pressure, shallow, underfloor plenums to provide plug-in electrical and communications raceways—just like home appliances—and highly efficient, warm and cool air directly to work stations.

Is it a Smart Building? Stewart Brand's *How Buildings Learn* is a useful primer of common sense case studies showing that buildings that have a long useful life are designed to easily accommodate and adapt to changes in use, culture, and technology, while many buildings designed for show or single purpose are not capable of learning and soon abandoned. With our clients, we often use the scenario planning approach to ask the unasked 'what if' questions regarding a building's adaptability to future programs and uses.

Is it User Friendly? A 'user friendly' building is designed for people first and recognizes that our bodies and sensing mechanisms are superbly designed to be tuned to natural cycles. Thirty years ago, progressive architects designed schools with no windows (to eliminate distractions—like clouds moving by the windows) and with high-intensity, evenly distributed fluorescent light (on the theory that students could read faster). In designing the Bateson State Office Building in Sacramento, the first major climate-responsive, energy-efficient office building, we rediscovered the obvious: what works in nature tends to work well for people. We are animals not machines, aren't we?

Does it Provide Better Environmental Performance? The measure here is the 'ecological footprint' of your building: all the impacts, direct and indirect, flowing from its sourcing, construction, and operation. The U.S. Green Building Council's LEED rating system is rapidly becoming a standard for assessing a building's impact on its site, the waste stream, pollution, indoor air quality, materials use, and energy efficiency. (See *www.usgbc.org* for more details.)

Does it Provide Better Economic Performance? We are often asked three basic questions: How much more does it cost to build green? How much longer does it take? How risky are the technologies? Following the information presented in this book and using the process outlined in these five points, we can confidently answer that doing it right costs no more, takes no longer, and adds no risk, although it provides an adventure! Carpenters are fond of saying, "measure twice, cut once!" That is what building with vision is all about.

Sim Van der Ryn is the founder of Van der Ryn Architects and the Ecological Design Institute in Sausalito, California. He can be contacted at www.vanderryn.com.

BUILDING WITH VISION

The Case for Local Solutions It has been said that one of the greatest scientific discoveries of the late 20th century is the fact that the Earth is a community, and that what happens to any part of that community also affects the whole. If this is true, and the Earth can only healthfully function as an interrelated and diverse community, it follows that our outlooks, approaches, and solutions must become more locally oriented. Considering the globalizing trends of cultures and economies, such an emphasis on community interdependence and local knowledge may seem outdated or even implausible. Yet creating diverse sets of local resources is among the greatest accomplishments we can achieve in the 21st century.

This realization of the importance of reviving vital, diverse communities comes at a time of unparalleled ecological threats. Global warming, species extinction, and pollution of all kinds are the byproducts of cultures increasingly addicted to faraway sources of basic necessities and luxury items, oblivious to how or by whom these products are created and what their real environmental and social costs are.

Consider contemporary residential construction. While many practices of yesteryear are happily forgotten, in the past 50 years we have strayed far and wide from the community approach of bygone eras. Materials and vernacular designs, once derived from local labor and resources and informed by regional climatic conditions, have become homogenized. It is as common to see Southwestern-inspired architecture outside the Southwest today as it is to find imported wood or stone featured in a region that is, or once was, abundant in local sources of both. It is even more increasingly common to find gigantic houses that don't blend in with either the landscape or the regional architecture and that are dependent upon consuming vast quantities of outside energy for heating, cooling, and electricity. We are living in the age of the industrial house, where traditions and limits seem no longer to apply. To build without a sense of history—of regional architecture or of the origins of the materials that go into a project—is to work in a vacuum without connection to place or future legacy.

Building A Vision: From Exploiters to Optimizers

This book, the second in a trilogy, is about building methods and materials, particularly those that optimize, minimize, or substitute for wood and wood products that are recycled or third party-certified 'well managed.' While its main focus is to present a conceptual overview of ways we might reduce our transgressions on the Earth's increasingly fragmented and diminished forests through our building projects, it also pertains to a larger movement in which many people are deeply engaged— that of restoring resourceful solutions to creating shelter. We are fortunate that the environmental building community has been actively growing and evolving in all parts of the country for well over three decades. Even though real progress in 'green' construction may just now be getting underway, a great many models, examples, resources, and products exist to reduce wood consumption, provide alternatives, improve materials use, and move us toward 'construction without destruction' and 'building as if forests mattered.' On the other hand, time is running out for the last of the Earth's great native forests, which can't afford to wait for the many generations it may take to create truly sustainable forestry and revive diverse building communities.

Presenting and addressing such a massive and complex issue as reducing wood consumption and creating more resourceful building approaches requires the participation of a wide range of people on a variety of levels—and by resourceful, we mean making full use of the chosen material and minimizing waste. Pioneers have already been trying for decades to change the course of 'building as usual.' One direction this exploration has taken is toward more highly processed building components such as steel studs, recycled plastics, engineered wood products, and manufactured housing. Another approach has been to revisit the past for modern solutions, using traditional and vernacular building methods in a present-day context. This book offers a broad overview of materials and approaches from both paths; not all of the ideas presented here will suit every philosophy. Advocates of 'natural building,' for example, may be unwilling to accept the use of styrofoam panel systems, despite their ability to significantly reduce a building's operational energy. At the same time, the extremely important and craftsman-like work being pioneered by natural builders—such as straw-bale, light straw clay, and rammed earth—won't trickle down to the general public without adaptations that substitute technology and mass production for hand labor to make them more affordable. These two seemingly opposed 'camps' are meeting with increasing frequency on the green building community's expanding playing field. Architects and builders are creating hybrid structures that combine both industrial materials and natural approaches in an attempt to balance aesthetic, code, performance, budget, and other considerations.

Any building project carries with it an ethical as well as aesthetic contract with society—as it requires resources first to be built and then maintained, restored, and eventually disposed of. Simply put, to build is to choose, and the choices can be complex and challenging. Each new home or remodel adds or detracts from the quality of life for its inhabitants, the local community, and the hundreds of places where the individual building components originated. In the best of all worlds, any new project would account for as many of the 'true costs' of building as possible. Were toxic chemicals involved in manufacturing? What impacts were created in the communities where raw materials were mined, harvested, or obtained? Does the building take advantage of the site's natural solar heating and cooling opportunities? Will the materials and building assembly produce a longlasting structure or one that will need quick replacement? Are local or regional materials and labor emphasized? While no one can have all the answers, anything short of trying to optimize with what we presently understand and continually asking deeper, more penetrating questions, is to fall short on the building's social contract with the community and the planet.

Green building is not the sole domain of idealists and artisans, nor is it only for the rich or environmentally minded. Rather, green building comprises the full aesthetic, economic, and ecological spectrum of contemporary building, from some of the country's most high-end buildings and residences to low-income redevelopment projects, such as the exemplary Casa Verde Program in Austin, Texas, or the reSourceful Building Project in Emeryville, California. It is in the spirit of presenting the broad scope of this work in a refreshing light that we have embarked upon this project.

We hope that builders, architects, property owners, and anyone undertaking a construction project will consider these ideas in the early phases of design and conceptualization, joining the party and inching us, one project at a time, a little closer toward building a vision, toward the highest possible quality of living for all of Earth's species.

A Concise View of Wood Use in America

It is easy perhaps to perceive resource depletion and land mismanagement as byproducts of 20th century economic industrialization and globalization, but the roots go back thousands of years. In North America, Europeans began burning and sawing their way through the continent's 850 million acres of ancient forests almost as soon as they arrived, annexing territory, establishing settlements and agriculture, constructing buildings, and providing raw materials for a burgeoning trade in ships and lumber. Ben Franklin wrote that by 1774, "wood, our common fuel which within these 300 years might be had at any man's door, must now be fetched near [160 kilometers] to some towns, and makes a considerable article in the expense of some families."[1] According to architectural historian Lester Walker, early colonists built with a variety of materials: wood in New England; brick in the Chesapeake Bay region; stone in the Delaware Valley; and numerous resources in the Hudson River Valley. Vernacular architecture evolved as local knowledge and materials bases grew. After the American Revolution, however, Walker writes that national and international influences began to supercede local knowledge. [2]

By the time President Thomas Jefferson dispatched Lewis and Clark to explore a route from the Missouri River to the Pacific

BASICS OF RESOURCE EFFICIENT BUILDING

Build small *Too often, building size is dictated by image and not by function. In the last three decades, the average American house size has increased while the number of people in a household has decreased; the average floor area per person rose from 427 to 756 square feet, or 77 percent.*

Pick a resource efficient location *Possibly the greatest construction-related harm to the natural environment and the greatest costs to governments, businesses, and individuals result from building on previously undeveloped land. Seek out sites in already-developed areas; consider rehabilitating or remodeling an existing structure.*

Design simply and elegantly *A great deal of wood and money is wasted on excess, such as unnecessarily complex roofs and appliqué decoration, instead of being invested in the design of timeless structures whose appeal relies on beautiful proportions and fine craftsmanship.*

Design for flexibility *A house that can accommodate a variety of household types, lifestyles, and functions is less likely to require remodeling than one that is designed for a narrowly defined market.*

'Open' building methods such as post-and-beam framing lend themselves most easily to adaptation.

Build for disassembly *Too often, the only way to get a building apart is with a wrecking ball, reducing valuable materials to rubble. Use screws and bolts, instead of glue and nails, whenever possible; avoid unrecyclable composites, especially those that are short-lived.*

Build a durable structure *Repair and replacement of deteriorating wood accounts for a significant percentage of the total demand for new wood. A well-detailed, solidly built house will outlive its shoddy counterpart by many years.*

Plan to minimize waste *Wasted materials are paid for twice: once to buy them, and again to dispose of them. Estimate carefully so you buy no more than you need; use materials to their fullest potential.*

Collaborate with the rest of your team *Opportunities for material efficiencies and time savings often can be found when the developer, architect, engineer, and builder combine resources. Set a meeting as early as possible in the project to discuss this goal.*

Reprinted with permission from *Efficient Wood Use in Residential Construction: A Practical Guide to Saving Wood, Money, and Forests*, by Ann Edminster and Sami Yassa.

Ocean, wood was consumed for fuel more than for any other purpose, while timber framing and log cabin building remained the norm in residential construction. According to author, teacher, and artisan builder Steve Chappell, that began to change in 1840 when a Shaker woman devised the circular saw blade, a technological innovation that eventually launched the revolution in stud- or stick-frame construction, which today accounts for at least 90 percent of residential buildings in the United States.[3] During the post-Civil War Reconstruction period, demand for quick, cheap housing rose dramatically. The circular saw's gains in speed and efficiency made it economically viable to cut smaller pieces of lumber which were far easier to transport, and thus provided construction materials to expand communities long after local resources had been depleted.

In some areas of the country, such as Nebraska and the Southwest, where access to wood was limited, construction methods using straw, sod, and adobe were developed. The story of late 19th century settlement and development in the United States is probably best summed up, however, by the myth of Paul Bunyan, the archetypical lumber jack who clearcut miles of forest with a swath of his axe and whose giant bovine sidekick, Babe, drank entire rivers dry in the taming of the wild West. By the close of the 19th century, one-third of the United States' forest land base had been liquidated. The Forest Service was established in 1897, with the express mission of protecting our forests from uncontrolled exploitation. But the idea that the forests provided irreplaceable benefits to the planet as a whole rather than just trees as a commodity resource—while advocated by visionaries like John Muir—fell prey to the engines of industrialization. Pressure in Congress soon increased to open the forests to timber

interests, and by 1899, the first commercial timber cutting began on National Forest land. In the years following, the logging industry and the Forest Service developed a cozy partnership. A recent editorial written by a coalition of forest activist organizations summarized the politics of 20th century industrial forestry this way: "Timber companies got a cheap wood supply, the Forest Service got a bloated budget from timber sales, and Congressmen got huge campaign donations from the industry."[4]

The post-World War II era saw an unprecedented growth in construction, inducing a lumber boom fueled by rapid changes in technology. According to Kathryn Kohm and Jerry Franklin: "By the 1950s, all new Bureau of Land Management and Forest Service timber sales in the Douglas fir region called for clearcutting. The result is a fragmented landscape in which species have been pushed to the edge of extinction, the productive capacity of many sites [has] been depleted, and public outcries have originated over landscape aesthetics."[5] Throughout the past 50 years, the timber industry has also shifted from manual labor to capital-intensive, mechanized technologies that have facilitated the extraction of massive volumes of trees on public and private lands. The amount of primary forest worldwide is now reported to be just 16 percent of its pre-industrial amount—and dwindling by the day.[6]

An Acre of Trees per House; Six Decks per Minute

It is estimated that an acre of forest—up to 44 trees—goes into the 12,500 board feet that make up the average 2,000-square-foot home in the United States. With approximately 1.5 million homes being built every year in the United States, this adds up to enormous pressure on the forests from residential construction and remodeling alone (not to mention paper, packaging, and fuel wood). In addition to wood products, the extraction of minerals and fuels needed for metals, glass, plastics, concrete, and other materials required to build the average house gouges out a crater equal to the size of the house itself, according to geologist John Wolfe.[7] And outpacing the early 21st century housing market's annual growth rate is the decking business, which completes six decks every minute in the United States, for a total of more than 3 million per year. Then there is the building industry's global footprint: 40 percent of the material resource and energy flows in the global economy are attributed to constructing or maintaining buildings. The global transportation of building materials and other related resources carries other impacts. Invasive diseases and organisms are regularly relocated via ship ballasts, raw logs, and other cargo, contributing to an escalating extinction crisis. With the broad-scale introduction of such exotic pests as the Asian long-horned beetle, the global logging and building trade carries with it serious threats to public and private forests.[8]

With only four percent of the United States' old-growth forests remaining, and wood consumption still rising, the forest products industry is resorting to the use of smaller, younger, trees each year. Quality lumber and plywood made from mature trees are being increasingly replaced by engineered products manufactured from chips and strands of adolescent or faster-growing, introduced, plantation species, bound together for strength with toxic substances that can negatively affect workers, homeowners, and habitats. The majority of chips come from virgin wood. In the southeastern United States alone, over 100 remote, high-capacity chip mills have been established within the last decade. Following 70 years of substantial regrowth in the region, the native forests are being rapidly transformed into clearcut, lunar landscapes, primarily serving the short-term interests of the global chip and paper pulp trade.[9] What's more, as a recent report published by The Pacific Forest Trust explains, forest industry carbon-emissions—largely the result of deforestation—are the second largest source of CO_2 emissions globally. At the same time, healthy forests represent our best chance to safely sequester CO_2, the most heavily emitted greenhouse gas. The authors argue that just the opposite management practices are needed to restore forest health and optimize our ability to store carbon—longer rotations, more selective cutting, and an augmented forest land base.[10]

Wood industry propaganda often touts the fact that there are more trees growing today than in bygone eras. In fact, the volume of timber harvests on private land outstripped tree growth throughout the 1980s and 1990s and is accelerating.[11] Another frequent industry claim is that industrial forestry practices, such as clearcutting, are beneficial for the forests because they mimic natural events, like fires and hurricanes, necessary for forests to regrow. These 20th century views have proven erroneous and indefensible. Most experts concur that industrial clearcuts do not generate the ecologically beneficial heat or ash that wildfires do, nor do they recreate soil conditions that often follow wind and ice storms. Fifty years of industrial logging, applying simple formulas over broad areas, has resulted in fragmented wildlife habitats, diminished water quality, the loss of heavy leaf and acorn production needed by many species, fisheries destroyed due to siltation and the loss of shade over streams. People living

SUMMARY OF PRODUCT STANDARDS FOR GREENSPEC

Building Green, based in Brattleboro, Vermont, keeps up to date with developments in the green building industry as earnestly as any organization in the country. Their resources and publications, thoroughly and rigorously researched, are a must for any green building library—including their monthly Environmental Building News newsletter and annual GreenSpec product resource guide. Below is a summary of the standards they use in choosing products for the GreenSpec. Contact www.buildinggreen.com for more information.

Products made from environmentally attractive materials
- *Salvaged products*
- *Products with post-consumer content*
- *Products with post-industrial content*
- *Certified wood products*
- *Rapidly renewable products*
- *Products made from agricultural waste material*
- *Natural or minimally processed products*

Products that are green because of what isn't there
- *Products that reduce material use*
- *Alternatives to ozone-depleting substances*
- *Alternatives to products made from PVC and polycarbonate*
- *Alternatives to conventional preservative-treated wood*
- *Alternatives to other components considered hazardous*

Products that reduce environmental impacts during construction, renovation, or demolition
- *Products that reduce the impacts of new construction*
- *Products that reduce the impacts of renovation*
- *Products that reduce the impacts of demolition*

Products that reduce environmental impacts of building operation
- *Building components that reduce heating and cooling loads*
- *Equipment that conserves energy*
- *Renewable energy and fuel cell equipment*
- *Fixtures and equipment that conserve water*
- *Products with exceptional durability or low maintenance requirements*
- *Products that prevent pollution or reduce waste*
- *Products that reduce or eliminate pesticide treatments*

Products that contribute to a safe, healthy, indoor environment
- *Products that don't release significant pollutants into the building*
- *Products that block development and spread of indoor contaminants*
- *Products that remove indoor pollutants*
- *Products that warn occupants of health hazards in the building*
- *Products that improve light quality*

Reprinted with permission from "Building Materials: What Makes a Product Green?" *Environmental Building News*, January 2001.

in forest communities realize that it's not the quantity of trees that matters, but the health of the ecosystems and watersheds that can sustain forests (and therefore forestry) over time. Large stands of diverse, older forests are far better able to survive natural events than are fragmented, fragile areas. They are also far better at storing carbon.[12] While important initiatives are underway to safeguard natural forests, it is clear today that we can't just have a few well-managed forests within entire zones of ecological sacrifice. Forests of the 21st century must be managed at the local level and be seamlessly connected to the larger landscape so that they can protect the breadth of biodiversity.

Wood: A Material of Choice?

Even with all of these ecologically urgent concerns of industrial forestry taken into account, it is important to emphasize that wood—sustainably managed, third party-certified, recycled, salvaged, or milled on-site—is often an appropriate material for building projects. Wood can create extremely durable structures and can require less fossil fuel energy to harvest and manufacture than many alternative materials. It can also be argued that wood building products store carbon as long as they remain in use.

There is no escaping, however, the implications of increasing human population growth coupled with intensifying global industrial development. Given our present appetite for and rampant waste of paper, packaging, and building materials, no management plans can hope to stem the overharvesting and losses of our forest ecosystems. Unless demand for forest resources is drastically reduced, we face a future far more bleak than what we know today. We face a future where a commonly asked question might be: "Is that *real* wood?"

Throughout the past ten years, the defense of our native forests has fallen on the shoulders of activists who often risk their lives doing the very jobs that our public officials and state and federal agencies are empowered to execute but often do not—thwarting logging practices and timber harvest plans that are ecologically destructive. With economic growth demands far outpacing the forests' natural abilities to recover, the pressure has almost become insurmountable. Fortunately, nonviolent protest and litigation are not our only options. Architects, builders, and consumers can join the movement as well, by looking for better sources of wood, by optimizing the use of the wood we do consume, and by using alternative materials and building methods.

Global Deforestation

Because the external costs of extraction and transportation are not reflected in the price of wood, it remains profitable to harvest timber from one side of the globe and ship it thousands of miles for use somewhere else. This early 1990s photo shows logs being exported from Longview, Washington. Imported old-growth materials from British Columbia, Southeast Asia, and the Amazon are frequently used in U.S. residential construction.

Lenses for Building with Vision

All buildings are endowed with some sense of vision. Building as if the forests matter requires some figurative time travel: foreseeing the impacts and outcomes of construction before the work takes place. Once underway, a construction project gathers a resource-consuming momentum all its own, like a marathon ride in a taxi cab with the meter running. The more extensive the research and advanced planning, the more control one has over the outcome. At the same time, it can be easy to dwell too much sometimes on details or one single charismatic material rather than on fundamental design issues. As the following discussion indicates, there are larger, systemic concerns at stake—such as the size of the house, its solar orientation, its operating energy needs, whether it is replacing versus remodeling a structure, its impact on the local watershed—that can be even more important than choices of materials or building methods. Details do matter, but keeping one's sights on the building's larger, overarching, environmental impacts, especially in the conceptual phase, is vital.

Most methods of assessing a building's environmental impacts attempt to create a 'life cycle analysis' of some sort. Such evaluations are perhaps more art than an exact science. And while there have been many attempts to create standards for what constitutes an environmentally acceptable material, a generally accepted authority is still lacking. Instead there are a few basic concepts that inform this complex decision making process.

First is the <u>materials perspective</u>: how and where they were sourced; whether or not any species were imperiled or ecosystems ravaged in their harvest or extraction; whether the raw materials are renewable or not; how much energy was required to produce them; whether or not they contain toxic or ozone-depleting chemicals; the effects of production, recycling, and disposal.

The amount of energy it takes to extract raw materials, transport them, then manufacture a product and install it is referred to as its <u>embodied energy</u>. Highly-processed standard building materials, such as steel, concrete, and aluminum, generally have a higher embodied energy than wood products. Recycled materials often (but not always) have less embodied energy than new materials. Salvaging and reusing buildings or their components and parts rather than starting again from scratch can substantially reduce the embodied energy of a building project. Moving toward natural building methods or traditional, local materials can also reduce the embodied energy of a project. Embodied energy values may even include factors like the transportation of laborers to the site.

A building's <u>operating energy</u> involves the total amount of energy the building consumes in its lifetime, including the energy supplied by utilities (or locally generated power and hot water) in order to maintain it. Factors such as building size, site orientation, engineering, and quality of insulation influence operating energy.

Fortunately, some general rules of thumb can help us make good decisions. According to the *Guide to Resource Efficient Building Elements*, "Environmentally aware builders, designers, and homeowners can usually identify building products with relatively low embodied energy. Building components made from recycled materials or minimally processed local materials tend to have less embodied energy than building products that are highly engineered, imported, or made from virgin resources. Choosing durable building products that require little maintenance will also help builders reduce the amount of embodied energy in a structure. It is only by addressing both components of energy usage—the operating and the embodied—that Americans can reduce the vast amount of energy consumed by buildings."[13]

Architect Larry Strain, of Siegel & Strain Architects in Emeryville, California, has developed a strategy for assessing green priorities for a given project, based on more than a decade of experience. "First we identify where the building's biggest impact will be," says Strain. "If it's a wood framed house we try to use FSC-certified products and use 'Optimum Value Engineering' to minimize the amount of framing materials required. On slab foundations, we try to maximize the amount of fly ash we can substitute for cement, which is energy-intensive and polluting. We often look at energy performance over time, and that can lead to some counter-intuitive decisions. For example, recycled cellulose insulation may have higher manufacturing impacts than a fiberglass product, but in the end, might perform far better by limiting air infiltration. A product such as fiber-cement siding might be energy-intensive to initially produce, but it also comes with as much as a 50-year warranty, making it a long-term option over wood siding that may last only 20 years."

Strain continues by differentiating between the priorities of a building's interior and exterior. "Inside a building, indoor air quality comes first, followed by resource impacts and durability. We avoid at all costs using carpets because they can severely compromise indoor air quality. The whole field of green construction is a continual learning process that improves one project at a time. We increasingly find ourselves trying to figure out big picture priorities, rather than tiny details."

Architect Gayle Borst, founder of the Austin-based firm Stewardship, Inc., chooses from a number of design options to optimize and substitute for wood. For interior partition walls, Borst regularly specifies light-gauge steel studs, autoclaved aerated concrete block or concrete block, straw board acoustical panels, or cob. Steel is also used for floor and roofing systems (with few thermal breaks) when she is not framing with certified wood studs spaced at 24 inches on center. Increasingly, Borst has been building with natural wall systems such as straw-bale, rammed earth, and cob, limiting wood to highly visible applications whenever possible. Numerous recycled wood items are incorporated into her projects as well, including salvaged doors, finger-jointed studs, and headers made from job site scrap.

Size Matters: Small, Tall, and Anti-Sprawl

Regardless of how thoughtful we are about materials or construction techniques, one of the best ways to minimize all of a building's environmental impacts is by designing smaller, more durable spaces. The average house size doubled between 1950 and 1990, with a present average of nearly 800 square feet of living space per person. Even while family size is diminishing, the floor area of new homes keeps growing. More than any other factor, square footage rather than quality or environmental impact defines the desirability and cost of development in virtually every real estate market in the country. Remnant woodlots, open space, and rural communities are the victims of this space and sprawl orgy.

Beyond environmental arguments, there are some obvious advantages to downsizing. The budget for durable materials and finishes can be upgraded, as can the fee for an architect to craft intelligent and utilitarian spaces. Building smaller can also potentially ease financial burdens, either by lightening the mortgage or by reducing heating and cooling costs over the life of the building. Small is not by definition always beautiful or material-efficient, however. A poorly designed small house can backfire, increasing stress and clutter. Increasing the complexity of the building design, particularly the perimeter, can also boost material use and labor cost.

Luckily, an increasing number of articles and books are appearing to chart these waters and offer many design tricks worthy of mention. Generous outdoor living spaces, such as covered porches, patios, gardens, and cooking areas, are one way to make smaller homes less restrictive and create usable space without excessive infrastructure and finishing. Inside, a number of moves can be made to give the illusion of big space in a small area, such as high ceilings and varied ceiling heights, incorporating subtle elevation changes to accentuate the differences between rooms. Creating built-in window seats, sleeping alcoves or lofts, sliding doors, bookshelves, and benches can also provide functional bonuses that make small living spaces more dynamic.

While building smaller homes is garnering increasing attention, perhaps an even more urgent need is to contain sprawling development. After all, even 'green' sprawl carves into vanishing open spaces, bringing with it roads, public services, and other infrastructure. While designing smaller homes is important, building taller structures in dense urban areas helps to contain construction impacts. Many resources in this book are suitable for multi-story buildings. Denser urban development can also be built to high standards of quality and aesthetics, as well as offering residents access to more amenities than sprawling suburbs do.

Projecting A Vision

What is the vision that this book sends out to the realm of residential builders? That the building of our homes becomes more responsive to our communities and regional resource bases. That the buildings we design and construct today truly merit their environmental costs many years from now, by enduring not just decades but centuries, by being totally recyclable, by optimizing the resources they do consume, or even by being made of materials that will innocuously return to the earth. That we continue to delve deeper into these complex issues and find ways, within every construction project, to build as if all forests mattered.

Chip Mountain

Throughout the 1990s, mountainous wood chip piles at the port in Puerto Montt, Chile have been continuously replenished for export. The country's endangered coastal temperate rainforests are a stunning testimony to the impacts of sustained export-driven forestry.

CERTIFIED

RECLAIMED

SALVAGED

For those of us who live in forested regions, wood will undoubtedly remain among our most important building resources. Fortunately, there is an increasing number of sources of environmentally preferable wood products, including FSC-certified products, recycled and salvaged timbers, formerly submerged logs, and materials from portable sawmill operators.

A healthy interest in sleuthing out the exact origins of materials is helpful in making sound choices about wood products. For example, if using virgin wood, did a credible outside organization monitor the harvesting conditions of the company or forest in question? Are you sure it isn't a threatened species or sold by a company known for logging in old-growth forests? If the wood is salvaged, under what conditions was the wood recovered?

Another useful and essential approach is to seek out local and regional suppliers of environmentally preferable building materials. The list of wood and architectural recycling companies is increasing rapidly, some of them include successful community-sponsored projects that put people to work and provide on-the-job training. As forests are increasingly depleted, formerly overlooked species ('lesser known species,' or 'LKS') are also coming to the forefront as good building options in many areas.

These very positive trends aside, the future health of our forests will still require a major overhaul of working forestry practices, a dramatic increase in restoration and the amount of 'forever wild' set-aside zones, all-out efforts to get the greatest use out of every piece of lumber that enters the building production stream, and the use and development of alternatives wherever appropriate.

Benefits: FSC often offers better quality wood than conventional suppliers. FSC requires third party, independent monitoring and clearly holds higher standards for sustainability than competing schemes. FSC holds the promise of establishing a forestry system that accounts for local and regional environmental conditions. FSC is widely acknowledged among the environmental community as the only credible certification program presently available for supplies of virgin wood materials from working forests.

Challenges: FSC-certified wood can be hard to find, resulting in higher costs and longer lead times. Activists have criticized FSC for certifying some companies on the basis of future promises rather than present practices—these cases will require careful monitoring. Standards for percentage-based products (such as paper, particleboard, etc., have been reduced to a 30 percent minimum, to be increased to 50 percent in 2005). Concerted efforts must be taken to protect streams and habitats (even within certified plantations), and to create set-asides, if FSC forests are to be functionally connected to larger ecosystems.

Applications: Framing lumber, interior plywood, flooring, siding, trusses, engineered wood products, doors, windows, cabinetry, furniture, decking, veneers, and particleboard. Work with suppliers and manufacturers to incorporate FSC wood in all aspects of construction.

WELL-MANAGED, WORKING FORESTS

First-hand familiarity with material sources—such as trees that have been harvested from the building site or from a local landowner whose harvesting or salvage practices you know something about—should always remain the highest form of 'certification.' While only a limited number of owners and builders have that opportunity, for other forest-conscious consumers there is FSC-certified wood. The acronym stands for Forest Stewardship Council, an international forest certification organization that has developed a system and standards to help ensure that logging and timber management activities protect the integrity of forests both during and after harvest. (The FSC stamp of approval is akin to shade grown coffee or organic food certification.) Rather than managing the forest like factory farms stocked with units of fiber, FSC sustainable forest management requires that working woodlands also provide other values, such as vital riparian zones and habitats healthy enough to support a breadth of native species. To that end, FSC performance standards include biodiversity, water quality, and economic and social responsibility criteria.

"A chain-of-custody, third party certification program starts in the forest and tracks the entire process from the forest through the mill or manufacturing plant, so that customers know their wood products came from verified sources," says Mark Comolli, of SmartWood, a Forest Stewardship Council certifying agency based in Richmond, Vermont. Through certification, motivation for responsible action shifts from government regulation (which continues to permit and even promote rampant ecological abuse of forests) to the marketplace, bringing consumers together with producers who demonstrate ecological, social, and economic responsibility.

The Uphill Rise of FSC

The movement toward developing sustainable forestry methods has been underway for decades, but only since the early 1990s has it become formalized on national and international levels. Headquartered in Oaxaca, Mexico, the FSC was founded in 1994 as an independent, non-profit, non-governmental organization fostering better forest management practices around the world.

Creating and maintaining a single set of standards to regulate a vast number of forest types, tree species, and climatic regions, as well as differing political, social, and economic priorities under which forests are managed has been no easy task. The FSC was created by a consensus process engaging environmental and social groups, consumer groups, and forest industry representatives. Together, these parties hammered out a set of principles and criteria for natural forest management and guidelines for certifiers. To date, nine accredited international organizations certify both natural forests and plantations, as well as the chain-of-custody (forest to manufacturer to retailer) of processed products and materials. As of December 2000, some 250 forests worldwide have been certified under the FSC umbrella, totaling 50 million acres, including nearly 8 million acres in North America.

Two organizations certify exemplary companies and individual foresters under the FSC program in North America: the Rainforest Alliance's Smart Wood program (based in Richmond, Vermont) and Scientific Certification Systems (of Oakland, California). FSC certification lasts five years, during which time companies agree to: maintain an open book policy, including maps and harvest plans; allow for spot inspections once per year; and respond satisfactorily to any complaints that may arise from the local community or government agencies.

A majority of the environmental community supports the Forest Stewardship Council program as an important and essential step toward the transformation of industrial forestry. Nonetheless, the movement has experienced its share of contention. U.S. activists, for example, have criticized FSC for permitting timber harvesting in state and national forests, a measure which conflicts with the Zero Cut on Public Lands campaign and the belief that the highest and best use of public forests lies in wilderness preservation. In many other countries, however, and Canada in particular (where a significant percentage of the forests are federally owned), this would prevent many legitimate woodlands and operations from becoming certified. The use of herbicides during post-harvest replanting remains another heated issue. While FSC certification does not allow aerial spraying of herbicides, ground-based applications of herbicides are permitted as a last resort, when ripping the soil or hand labor becomes prohibitively expensive in replanting stands of trees. Yet another criticism alleges that some companies have been certified based on proposed long-term improvements rather than established on-the-ground management practices.

In developing accreditation standards that reflect the complexity and diversity of forest systems, FSC established a list of ten golden rules or principles that apply to all producers, no matter

FSC's Ten Principles of Forest Stewardship

1. Meet all applicable laws and FSC Principles.

2. Have legally established, long-term forest management rights.

3. Recognize and respect the rights of indigenous peoples.

4. Maintain the economic and social well-being of local communities.

5. Conserve the forests' economic resources.

6. Protect biological diversity.

7. Have a written management plan.

8. Engage in regular monitoring and assessment.

9. Conserve primary forests and well-developed secondary forests.

10. Manage plantations so as to alleviate pressures on natural forests.

Visit *www.fscus.org* for the extended version of these principles.

where the forests are located (see page 26). To supplement those general standards, FSC initiated a process of establishing regional criteria to account for different forest types and climatic conditions and differing social and economic contexts. In the United States, 11 separate groups are now developing specific regional standards.

FSC has also set an unusual precedent by moving beyond woodlot certification to endorsing all timber management done by exemplary foresters. In one such case, recognizing that the forests managed by Craig Blencowe of Fort Bragg, California, consistently exceeded FSC standards, SmartWood, together with the Willits, California-based Institute for Sustainable Forestry, granted certification to any of the woodlots Blencowe manages—without the need for independent inspection of each logging operation. Similar certifications have been awarded to foresters in many regions of the country. This allows stewardship-minded property owners to hire certified foresters to manage their woodlots under FSC guidelines without the financial burden of paying for certification.

Builder Advantages

From the builder or homeowner point of view, FSC offers, first and foremost, a sense of satisfaction that the project is being built with wood produced to a higher standard of accountability that is absent from conventional forestry. The FSC stamp carries with it the means of connecting wood products to a functioning ecosystem.

Quality can be another key advantage. "People should consider buying FSC because it's a higher quality product," says Wade Mosby, Vice President of Marketing for Collins Pine, one of the country's largest FSC suppliers with nearly 300,000 certified acres in California and Pennsylvania. "Ours are industrial forests—but not plantations—and we're working on 140-year rotations with a lot less impacts," Mosby says of his company's forestry operations. "The resulting product really shows in a clearer, tighter grain. Right now, there is not even much of a premium for FSC-certified wood, and any extra costs are more than made up for in quality and performance." For companies that have been practicing long-term management for decades (such as Collins Pine, Menominee Tribal Enterprises, and Big Creek Lumber) FSC certification can involve forests with much longer harvest rotations, which yield older, straighter wood. Straighter wood means fewer on-site rejections and a tighter building envelope overall. Using lumber that doesn't warp or twist lessens the chance of gaps developing in the framing structure, which can compromise energy efficiency and comfort as well as the durability of a building.

Not all FSC-certified forests possess the same qualities as those mentioned above, however. With millions of additional acres being certified each year, the FSC industry now offers a wide variety of products derived from a range of forests. Depending on where you live, FSC-certified dimensional lumber and framing timbers, plywood, finish products, particleboard, and paper products are all available. Products and suppliers can be researched on a number of websites (see page 38), such as the Certified Forest Products Council based in Portland, Oregon (*www.certifiedwood.org*).

Depending on their project's location, architects and

builders can specify certified materials from custom manufacturers of almost any product, from doors and windows to structural members. On a recent project for the East Bay Regional Park District, architect Larry Strain tried to purchase microlams made from FSC-certified wood. "There was a timing problem so we couldn't get them for this project," Strain explained. "Instead, we paid the supplier the price difference and in return they agreed to purchase the equivalent amount of FSC-certified wood and incorporate it into their material stream."

Building the Market—Chicken or Egg?

Among the first North American distributors of FSC-certified wood products was EcoTimber of Berkeley, California. Started in 1992 by partners Jason Grant, Eugene Dickey, and Aaron Maizlish, EcoTimber has slowly and steadily built a multi-million dollar distribution business, establishing a reputation for 'good woods' ranging from FSC-certified to reclaimed lumber to urban and rural salvage. EcoTimber has also been innovative in offering framing packages to contractors as well as quality woods for furniture, cabinetry, millwork, and even musical instruments. EcoTimber has recently chosen to specialize in FSC-certified flooring, decking, and garden furniture.

The most significant catalyst to increasing both the acreage of FSC-certified timber land as well as the mainstream availability of FSC products could be Home Depot's late 1999 declaration that it would discontinue carrying old-growth products in its stores by 2002 and simultaneously phase in FSC supply. That announcement was followed by its competitor Lowes' decision in summer 2000 to aggressively phase out wood products from endangered forest areas, such as the Great Bear Rainforest of British Columbia. Both companies have expressed their support for FSC-certified products, which could vastly improve availability to customers throughout the country. Following Lowes' and Home Depot's leads, many other home improvement retailers are pledging to phase out old-growth wood and incorporate FSC-certified wood in their product lines.

"Home Depot and Lowes have lit a fire under suppliers," says Hank Cauley, executive director of Washington, D.C.-based FSC-U.S. "These companies are taking a leadership role in terms of supplying the country with the best standards available. Now it's up to us to increase the number of suppliers, the number of highly

Model Remodel

When the Foundation for Deep Ecology converted a former barracks into its non-profit headquarters, great care was given to material selection. FSC studs and plywood were chosen for framing and sheathing. Wood paneling was salvaged from a turn-of-the-century factory. Workstations were refashioned from old institutional chairs and desks. Original wood windows were repaired and upgraded. Cabinets were crafted from FSC-certified Douglas fir sinker logs. (SKA Architects, San Francisco.)

THE FSC-CERTIFIED HAYWARD TRUSS

The advantages of premanufactured roof trusses in appropriate projects include: less expensive than stick-framed rafters, less overall wood use, and less jobsite waste. What has been lacking, however, is a steady supply of roof trusses and other engineered wood products made from FSC-certified raw materials. In April 2000, Hayward Truss of Santa Maria, California introduced the country's first FSC-certified trusses. (Hayward Truss is a subsidiary of Monterey, California-based Hayward Lumber Company, one of the West Coast's leading suppliers of FSC-certified framing lumber.) Due to a reliable flow of materials, FSC-certified Douglas fir trusses can now be made as easily as their conventional counterparts.

"If we are going to build the future—in both the literal and the figurative sense—we need to learn to build sustainably," explains Peter Nowack, Hayward Lumber's Director of Marketing and Sustainability. "The use of FSC-certified framing lumber and trusses reduces a home's environmental footprint, protects the values of the forest, and delivers off-site benefits that range from habitat and biodiversity protection, to ensuring clean air and water for this and future generations."

The company's first certified trusses were incorporated into the Wolken Sustainability Center in Palo Alto, California. As more people learn about the benefits of FSC-certified wood, Hayward expects that certified trusses will become an important component of the West Coast construction industry. Since the Hayward truss doesn't cosmetically appear to be any different from a conventional truss, users need to look to the certified forests and the communities in which they are located to find the added value. Over time, FSC management practices should help to balance environmental, economic, and social interests.

For more information, contact *www.haywardgreen.com.*

FSC AT SFO

When Skidmore, Owings, and Merrill Architects (SOM) were designing the new main terminal at San Francisco's International Airport, they envisioned a cherry veneer panel 670 feet long and 38 feet high to complement a primarily glass and steel atrium of monumental proportions. Louis Buchner, of the San Francisco-based Architectural Forest Enterprises (now Vida), encouraged SOM to specify FSC-certified veneer to make a powerful positive public statement.

"Time was a critical factor in meeting the strict quality and color specifications required by the architects," remembers Buchner. "With a one-year lead time, there was ample opportunity to source material. And in the end, certified veneer emerged as the same price and quality level as its conventional competitors."

Thirty trees, halved, then thinly sliced, provided the material for the installation. Non-certified, fire-rated particleboard served as the substrate, with low-grade FSC-certified cherry backing each panel.

qualified certifiers, and to work for continuous improvement in reversing the practice of poor forest management."

SFI—The Fox Guarding the Hen House

Not all 'certification' programs are created equal. FSC's most significant opposition has come from the U.S. forest products industry, whose Sustainable Forestry Initiative (SFI) is a set of voluntary, self-enforcing guidelines. Created by the American Forest and Paper Association, in the mid-1990s, the major trade group for forest and paper interests, in response to increasing criticism of conventional forestry practices across the country, SFI has been promoted through a costly industrywide campaign.

The SFI guidelines state that members must develop specific programs, plans, and policies to achieve sustainability. The catch is that SFI doesn't tell companies what to do, or how much, in order to enhance wildlife habitat, ensure prompt reforestation, or foster biodiversity. It doesn't describe specific goals that companies must meet in the field, nor does it require any third party enforcement mechanism. To the detriment of consumers who really want to support better forest practices, the industry-sponsored SFI adopts the language of environmental protection, but lacks the bite of the FSC. In effect, it serves as little more than a marketing device to encourage the consumption of status-quo forest products.

"In terms of the performance standards and acceptance by the environmental community of the current forest management certification systems," explains SmartWood marketing manager Mark Comolli, "on a scale of 1 through 10, FSC is an 8. SFI is a 2."

From Certification to Sustainability?

The potential for the development of local or regional supplies of environmentally-certified wood products has captured the imagination of many people. In tandem with other wood-saving innovations and practices, worldwide adoption of FSC standards could help us to move closer to more resourceful building. But the question remains: will the mainstreaming of FSC really get us on the path to sustainability?

In *The Natural Step for Business* (New Society, 1999) authors Brian Natrass and Mary Altomare interviewed Jim Quinn, ex-President and CEO of the FSC pioneering company, Collins Pine. Quinn stated his position that a truly regenerative timber industry could offer ecological advantages over many alternative building materials, such as concrete, steel, and plastics. "Those materials rely on non-renewable raw materials and use significant amounts of non-renewable energy in their production. Trees, however, are renewable. The real challenge," Quinn pointed out, "is clarifying the difference between renewability and sustainability. A sustainable forest manager allows the trees to renew themselves. But that's only one part of it. The other side is that while you're managing the forest, you still have a conscious awareness of, and a focus on, biological systems and diversity such that you don't take all the trees out at once and deprive everything that lives there of their habitat. So you do a little bit at a time."

In other words, FSC is a valuable intermediary step, worthy of our support, but also in need of close scrutiny. Hopefully in the long run, FSC will serve as the springboard for deeper, sweeping, and significant change.

FROM THE FOREST TO THE FLOOR

Thirteen years ago, Jim Birkemeier began actively unlearning what he had been taught in forestry school. "As a conventional forester, you are taught to feed the industry with cheap timber," says Birkemeier, an FSC-certified forester and owner of Timbergreen Forestry in Spring Green, Wisconsin. The practice of continually 'high-grading'—taking the best trees in a stand and leaving the rest—has gravely depleted the capacity for the Lake States forests to supply quality lumber. Birkemeier turned to FSC practices as an alternative model of forest stewardship. "Managing our forests for the long term requires that we leave the good trees standing for decades and develop markets for the small, damaged, and dying in the short term," says Birkemeier. To that end, Timbergreen began developing value-added products. Today the company harvests, manufactures, sells, and installs FSC-certified character grade flooring from red oak and lesser known species such as big tooth aspen. "Each floor we install sells another," says Birkemeier. Customers as far as six hours away are paying premiums for Timbergreen's FSC certification and rustic quality.

Based on his success, Birkemeier has been gradually organizing regional landowners to increase the supply and acreage of FSC-certified materials in the Midwest. To date, the Sustainable Woods Cooperative includes 140 landowners and 20,000 acres within a 50-mile radius of Lone Rock, Wisconsin. "We've shown that sustainable practices and products are profitable on our farm, and there is a high interest among people looking for a better way to manage their lands," says Birkemeier.

For more information contact *www.timbergreenforestry.com* and *www.sustainablewoods.com*.

Benefits: Can obtain fine materials with old-growth characteristics that have long since been harvested. Prevents perfectly usable materials from being chipped or going to the landfill. Alleviates pressure for virgin wood. Can be sourced regionally in many cases. Offers aesthetic character and sometimes structural values that are often hard to come by in virgin wood products.

Challenges: Working with reclaimed wood often requires additional labor in sorting, milling, or carpentry. Costs can be higher than virgin wood. For wood salvaged from local forests, verify that habitat disturbance is minimized. Supplies are presently abundant, but limited in the long term.

Applications: Siding, post-and-beam members, and other structural lumber. Flooring, decking, cabinetry, doors, windows, railings, entire floors and many other categories can be salvaged and reused.

Portable Mini-Mill

San Luis Obispo salvage operator Don Seawater at work at his Wood-Mizer. Seawater makes his living converting urban blow downs, driftwood, and other casualties into quality timbers and lumber.

WHAT LASTS SHOULD COME FIRST

There are few materials that rival the beauty, integrity, and durability of old-growth timbers. They have allowed us to make historic barns, houses, and other buildings; irreplaceable musical instruments; and exceptional furniture. The timber of old-growth trees is harder, denser, and more stable, and has fewer knots and structural defects than that of young trees. However, old-growth timber primarily comes from ancient forests, which, with only a few rare and notable exceptions, such as the FSC-certified lands of the Menominee Tribal Enterprises, should be placed under permanent protection.

It is still possible, however, to purchase reclaimed and salvaged wood from reputable sources to obtain the benefits of old-growth timber. Old-growth lumber is currently being reclaimed from old warehouses, buildings, bridges, brewing tanks, and other structures undergoing deconstruction—and indications are that billions of board feet of reusable wood resources exist across the U.S. and Canada.[1] Logs are also being salvaged from lakes, urban woodlots, and rural areas, where oversight, blow-downs, disease, or insect infestations present opportunities to convert raw materials into lumber.

Reclaimed and salvaged lumber has a number of advantages. For the most part, the environmental costs of harvesting these materials have already taken place. At a time when global forests are under increasing deforestation pressures, reusing wood can reduce the need for virgin timber. According to the Natural Resources Defense Council's Efficient Wood Use in Residential Construction, for example, an old warehouse with 1 million board feet of reusable lumber can offset the need to harvest one thousand acres of trees.[2]

Because of the era in which it was originally harvested, salvage lumber is often tightly grained old-growth wood. Having stood in the open air many years, reclaimed wood is dry and has a stable moisture content that will prevent further warping and twisting. As with other resources, the supply of reclaimed wood is limited, however. Efficient and appropriate use of reclaimed wood is important for its long-term availability. As many architects and designers recommend, wood with such exceptional character should be featured in highly visible applications.

Among the very first things builders and homeowners can do when planning any project is to identify potential uses for and sources of locally salvaged wood. Recovered wood, such as flooring, siding, and other custom milled products, are sometimes even advertised in classified newspaper ads. If none is available locally, look to regional and national suppliers. (See pages 38-39 for a detailed list of websites.)

Within the past 15 years, wood recycling has gone from cottage industry to the mainstream. Products often (though not necessarily) come at a premium, and are likely to remain beyond the reach of many builders on a tight budget. One of the primary sources of materials are industrial buildings, including warehouses, mills, and manufacturing facilities of the 19th and early 20th centuries. In the late 1990s, more than 650 companies were providing recycled wood for building applications, an industry segment that appears to be growing. The decommissioning of military buildings throughout the country could free up hundreds of millions of board feet of old-growth lumber for a variety of applications.[3]

"For at least the next ten years, the reclaimed lumber market will be strong," predicts Erica Carpenter, co-founder of Jefferson Recycled Woodworks, a nationwide distributor of reclaimed wood products based in McCloud, California.

According to Carpenter, "reclaimed lumber isn't a practical choice for the average householder who needs just a few pieces for a shelving unit or small project." However, larger items such as structural timbers for framing, boards for floors, or materials for fine cabinetry make reclaimed wood an excellent option. Any nail holes, bolt holes, fastener marks or wear—while they can undoubtedly require additional labor—are part of the appeal of these materials.

Wildfire Wood

A tragic wildfire in the Santa Lucia Range created the opportunity for rebuilding the home and office of architects Ken Haggard and Polly Cooper, of the San Luis Sustainability Group. Using materials milled from burned logs, they built post-and-beam and straw-bale infill stuctures with wood surfaces on floors, ceilings, stairs, countertops, trim, and railings. The diverse species mix included Sargent cypress, red alder, California bay, Douglas fir, and others.
See www.slosustainability.com for more details.

"Reclaimed wood has distinct performance and environmental advantages over green old-growth material that is still being harvested under disastrous conditions," says Carpenter. First, it is dry. Reclaimed wood is also often available in species, coloration, and quality not found in today's forests.

Wood is also being salvaged from urban woodlots, orchards, forests, and, in some cases, river and lake bottoms (known as 'sinkers' from the bygone era of river- and lake-based logging.) This form of salvage does not entail cutting dead trees from the forest because of their merchantability (which has been the source of considerable protest by the environmental community), but rather the recovery of trees that have been cut long ago. Some, but not all, of these kinds of salvaged materials are FSC-certified. (Richmond, Vermont-based SmartWood, for example, has a Rediscovered Wood program). Because retrieving logs either from the forest floor or aquatic areas sometimes involves some habitat disturbance, a blanket stamp of approval on all salvage materials is not appropriate. Decaying old-growth logs and snags also play an essential role in forest ecology. When purchasing salvaged wood, it is especially important to verify the circumstances under which it was obtained.

Arborist Brian Usilton has spent more than a decade as an independent miller of redwood logs that were felled decades ago in the Anderson Valley of Mendocino County, California, but were never hauled out of the woods and converted into lumber. Loggers frequently left the larger, less uniform sections of the old-growth trees lying in the woodlot, focusing instead on the straighter, more manageable and marketable sections of the trunks. Many of these logs remain in surprisingly good condition where they were abandoned, although

a decade of steady use by a number of salvage operators has made the best-quality wood harder to come by.

Usilton acknowledges what many people in the reclaimed lumber industry know about the salvaged wood market. It is a limited resource, with few regional areas, such as the north coast of California and Pacific Northwest, that can be developed. Even so, he has been able to consistently find enough logs to salvage clear, old-growth 1x10 and 1x3 board-and-batten siding for six to nine houses per year. His salvage operation is relatively small: a Wood-Mizer bandsaw mill, a heavy-duty logging truck, and an assortment of other log transporting devices and accessories. Nearly every board he mills is sold to homeowners in the local area and all of the products and by-products of the old logs are used, either as lumber, kindling, or compost (in the case of sawdust).

Other sources of salvaged old-growth redwood have included 'sinkers' and 'runaways,' which bounded into inaccessible areas after felling. For a time, scuba divers were hauling sinkers out of California's rivers, a practice that has been banned to preserve much-needed pools for fish habitat. There are still estimated to be billions of board feet of environmentally acceptable salvaged old-growth wood in waters throughout North America, where scuba salvaging continues and is sometimes FSC-certified. Helicopters are sometimes used to hoist runaways out of steep canyons, a practice that seems unjustifiably energy-intensive.

Green Mountain Wild Woods in Woodstock, Vermont specializes in salvaging, disease-killed butternut, a species under attack in the Northeast by an airborne fungus. A lesser-known relative of the black walnut, the butternut

97 PERCENT RATE OF RETURN:
THE ECOTRUST NATURAL CAPITAL CENTER

When preparing to renovate the century-old timber and masonry Rapid Transfer Building, a shipping and storage depot along the Willamette River in downtown Portland, Oregon, the non-profit group Ecotrust was seeking an unusual rate of return. "Our goal was to recycle all demolition materials and to rebuild the new Natural Capital Center using 100 percent salvaged or FSC-certified woods," says project director Bettina von Hagen. "Unfortunately, we fell a few percent short when we had to buy non-certified plywood because the only producer of structural plywood closed its plant. Other than that," she continues, "we believe this might be the highest level of recycling on any renovation project in the country."

For the folks at Ecotrust, who spearheaded this 11-million-dollar warehouse renovation, recycling was never an economic question. According to Carrington Barrs of the Walsh Construction Company, recycling the wood from both structures penciled out quite well, even considering that careful deconstruction took twice as long as a more conventional demolition approach.

Ecotrust removed a two-story annex that was in disrepair, with the intention of reusing the old beams and other salvageable materials to build a third-story addition to house the Certified Forest Products Council. (Other demolition materials were sold to recycling brokers; only five debris boxes were hauled away during the course of a year.) Ecotrust was also fortunate that an adjacent structure was being torn down simultaneously, offering a treasure trove of materials.

"First, the demolition of this old post-and-beam and masonry building lent itself to careful recovery of the materials," Barrs explains. "We were already on site and without too much trouble or damage, we could carefully remove the old timbers, to be reused later free of charge. The timbers recovered on the adjacent lot were available to us at 55 cents per board foot. First of all, we couldn't find this kind of wood, unless it was old-growth. Secondly, the glulams and microlams that would have replaced them were far more expensive."

The finished project will include the reuse of existing brick and timber materials, seismic improvements, an energy-efficient HVAC system, daylighting, operable windows, and one of Portland's first living roofs.

For more information, see www.ecotrust.org.

was long prized for its delicious nuts, rather than wood values, and for that reason was an overlooked timber species. It is, however, a very rot-resistant softwood, suitable for numerous architectural milling applications as well as flooring. The company only buys trees dead in the forest from regional foresters, but is currently not FSC-certified. "Worms are my signature of credibility when buying a log," says Parker Nichols, founder of the company. "Powderpost beetles only infest sick or dead trees and their trails are readily traceable. I also keep specific harvest records of where the trees came from." As a Category Two threatened species, it is illegal to cut live butternut on public lands, and Green Mountain Wild Woods reports refusing all opportunities to procure live trees on private lands. Nichols estimates at least a decade of regionally sourced supply exists due to the devastating plight of the butternut.

Author's Residence

For their Mendocino County home, Building with Vision *author Dan Imhoff and his wife Quincey searched out regional materials. FSC-certified Douglas fir was obtained for most framing; salvaged redwood posts and board-and-batten siding were provided by a local arborist; and, in the photo at left, a recycled fir floor was chosen when an outdoor breezeway was renovated into a den.*

As you start project planning, ask your contractor, local hardware store, or lumber supplier about the availability of FSC-certified, recycled, and salvaged materials, and allow yourself some lead time. With a little bit of legwork and some flexibility, almost anything can be custom-made using FSC-certified products, from complete framing packages, to windows and doors, to manufactured trusses and floor systems. With the commitment of major hardware chains to offer FSC-certified forest products across the country, we can expect to find increasing numbers of items, product lines, and private labels as standard stock. Liberty Valley Doors, in Cotati, California, the largest door manufacturer in the northern part of the state, regularly produces custom doors from FSC wood in response to requests from Bay Area architects. Certified wood distributor EcoTimber in Berkeley, California, has launched its own private label of flooring products. Colonial Craft in Minneapolis has been pioneering the use of certified wood in their lines of high performance, energy-efficient windows and doors (as used in the Ecotrust Natural Capital Center—see page 35). Anderson Windows has also committed to injecting FSC wood into their materials stream, although they have no 100 percent certified product as of this printing. Collins Pine will soon introduce FSC-certified hardboard siding. Consider also specifying 'character grade' rather than 'clear' FSC-certified woods for many applications—a little aesthetic flexibility will contribute to a more thorough use of forest resources. Don't forget that finish surfaces, cabinetry, and trim can all be made from FSC-certified and recycled materials as well. (See pages 116-117 for more examples.)

(See pages 116-117 for more examples.)

Forest Activist Organizations

AMERICAN LANDS ALLIANCE
Washington, DC
202.547.9400
www.americanlands.org

DOGWOOD ALLIANCE
Asheville, North Carolina
828.698.1998
www.dogwoodalliance.org

FOREST ETHICS
Berkeley, California
510.533.8725
www.forestethics.org

FOREST TRENDS
Washington, D.C.
202.530.2020
www.forest-trends.org

GLOBAL FOREST WATCH
Washington, DC
202.729.7600
www.globalforestwatch.org

GREENPEACE
Washington, DC
800.326.0959
www.greenpeaceusa.org

NATIVE FOREST NETWORK
Missoula, Montana
406.542.7343
Burlington, Vermont
802.863.0571
www.nativeforest.org

NATURAL RESOURCES DEFENSE COUNCIL
New York, New York
212.727.2700
San Francisco, California
415.777.0220
www.nrdc.org

RAINFOREST ACTION NETWORK
San Francisco, California
415.398.4404
www.ran.org

FSC Supplier Information

CERTIFIED FOREST PRODUCTS COUNCIL
Beaverton, Oregon
503.590.6600
www.certifiedwood.org
moving to Portland, August 2001

FOREST STEWARDSHIP COUNCIL U.S.
Washington. D.C.
202.342.0413
www.fscus.org

FORESTWORLD
Shelburne, Vermont
802.865.1111
www.forestworld.com

Forest Certification Programs

SCIENTIFIC CERTIFICATION SYSTEMS
Oakland, California
510.832.1415
www.scs1.com/forestry.shtml

SMARTWOOD
Richmond, Vermont
802.434.5491
www.smartwood.org

EARTHSOURCE FOREST PRODUCTS
Locations in Northern California
510.549.9663
www.earthsource.com

ECOTIMBER
Berkeley, California
510.549.3000
www.pals4wood.com

ENDURA WOOD PRODUCTS
Portland, Oregon
503.233.7090
www.endurawood.com

ENVIRONMENTAL BUILDING SUPPLIES
Portland, Oregon
503.222.3881

ENVIRONMENTAL HOME CENTER
Seattle, Washington
206.682.7332
www.built-e.com

HARWOOD PRODUCTS
Willits, California
707.459.5595

HAYWARD LUMBER
Pacific Grove, California
831.646.8184
www.haywardgreen.com

MATHEUS LUMBER COMPANY
Woodinville, Washington
800.284.7501
www.matheuslumber.com

NORTHLAND FOREST PRODUCTS
New Hampshire and Virginia
603.642.3665

PLAZA HARDWOOD
Santa Fe, New Mexico
800.662.6306
www.plzfloor.com

Also contact local home improvement retailers such as Home Depot, Lowes and Lumberman's (in the Northwest).

CAPITAL LUMBER
7 locations in the west
602.381.0709
www.capital-lumber.com

CERTIFIED WOOD SOURCE
Glendale, Arizona
623.582.0490

CHALLINOR WOOD PRODUCTS
Wilmette, Illinois
847.256.8828

EDENSAW WOODS
Port Townsend, Washington
800.745.3336
www.edensaw.com

FOREST PLYWOOD SALES
La Mirada, California
714.523.1721
www.forestplywood.com

GREEN MOUNTAIN WOODWORKS
Phoenix, Oregon
541.535.8304

KHEOPS FOREST PRODUCTS
Quebec City, Canada
418.627.2773
www.kheopswood.com

LUMBER PRODUCTS
Portland, Oregon
503.692.3322
www.lumberproducts.com

SUSTAINABLE WOODS COOPERATIVE
Lone Rock, Wisconsin
608.583.7100
www.sustainablewoods.com

SYLVANIA CERTIFIED
Santa Fe, New Mexico
800.468.6139

www.buildfind.com
Enter 'salvage wood' in their Search function. Over 200 listings appear by company and product. Listings link directly to recycled lumber dealers web site. At the time of review, you could not search by state, city or company.

www.recycle.net/Wood/index.html
Lists wood by categories: used/reusable lumber and wood, lumber grades, and products made from recycled wood. Listings link directly to suppliers' web sites.

www.harrisdirectory.com
Comprehensive information on recycled wood and other products. Paid service: $150 annual subscription to searchable updated database on recycled wood product suppliers. Can search by city, state, company name, and environmental benefits.

www.crbt.org
Center for Resourceful Building Technology E-guide lists companies with different recycled wood products.

www.woodwise.org or
www.coopamerica.org/woodwise/wdirectory.html
Lists both recycled and FSC-certified wood suppliers under 'Home Improvement Supplies.'

www.woodfibre.com
Listings under Lumber Industry for used and reusable lumber.

www.oldhousejournal.com
Site for the Old House Journal Restoration Directory. Includes alphabetized listing of salvage wood companies.

www.buildinggreen.com
This is the site of the *Environmental Building News* newsletter and GreenSpec environmental products and services guide.

www.crest.org
An important site for general green building information, including sustainable technologies and renewable energy.

www.greenclips.com
This site has traditionally featured excellent reports on the green building and environmental business communities.

www.usgbc.org
The U.S. Green Building Council on-line site offers a number of excellent green building resources, including tools like LEED and BEES.

www.eco-labels.org
The Consumers Union lists and evaluates numerous eco-labeling programs for food and wood products.

Recycled Wood Suppliers

Search out local suppliers of recycled and salvaged wood and other building materials in your area. The yellow pages and classifieds can be good places to start. There is an ever-increasing contingent of companies and community-based organizations specializing in building salvage, and portable sawmill operators willing to come to your site to cut custom lumber.

BLACK'S FARM WOOD
San Rafael, California
877.321.WOOD
www.blacksfarmwood.com

ENVIRONMENTAL TIMBER RECOVERY
Vancouver, British Columbia
604.434.0465
finewood@uniserve.com

JEFFERSON RECYCLED WOOD-WORKS
McCloud, California
530.964.2740
www.ecowood.com

MAXWELL PACIFIC
Malibu, California
310.457.4533

MOUNTAIN LUMBER COMPANY
Ruckersville, Virginia
800.445.2671

PINOCCHIO'S LUMBER COMPANY
Fort Bragg, California
707.964.6272
www.mcn.org/b/rmoore/

REUSABLE LUMBER COMPANY
Woodside, California
650.529.9122
www.reusablelumber.com

TRESTLEWOOD
Blackfoot, Idaho
877.375.2779
www.trestlewood.com

THE WOODS COMPANY
Chambersburg, Pennsylvania
717.263.6524
www.thewoodscompany.com

Arsenic- and Chromium-free Treated Wood

CHEMICAL SPECIALTIES, INC.
Charlotte, North Carolina
704.522.0825
www.treatedwood.com

Resource Guides

THE ALTERNATIVE BUILDING SOURCEBOOK
Fox Maple Press
Brownfield, Maine
207.935.3720
www.foxmaple.com

ARCHITECTURAL RESOURCE GUIDE
ADPSR West Coast
Berkeley, California
510.273.2428
www.adpsr-norcal.org has an out-standing listserv for the Northern California region.

GREENSPEC: The Environmental Building News Product Directory and Guideline Specifications
E Build, Inc.
Brattleboro, Vermont
800.861.0954
www.greenspec.com
Order directory at www.building-green.com

GUIDE TO RESOURCE EFFICIENT BUILDING ELEMENTS
Center for Resourceful Building Technology
Missoula, Montana
406.549.7678
www.crbt.org

THE HARRIS GUIDE
Santa Fe, New Mexico
www.harrisdirectory.com

WOOD WISE CONSUMER GUIDE
Resource Conservation Alliance
Washington, D.C.
202.387.8030
www.rca-info.org/consumer-guide.html

EFFICIENT WOOD USE IN RESIDENTIAL CONSTRUCTION: A Practical Guide to Saving Wood, Money, and Forests
Ann Edminster and Sami Yassa, Natural Resources Defense Council (NRDC)
New York, New York
212.727.2700
www.nrdc.org

BUILDING WITH ALTERNATIVES TO LUMBER AND PLYWOOD IN HOME CONSTRUCTION AND COST-EFFECTIVE HOME BUILDING
National Association of Home Builders Research Center
Upper Marlboro, Maryland
301.249.4000/800.638.8556
www.nahbrc.org

Community-Oriented Salvage Programs

COMMUNITY WOODWORKS
Oakland, California
510.835.7690

REBUILDING CENTER
Portland, Oregon
503.331.1877

SUSTAINABLE NORTHWEST HEALTHY FORESTS HEALTHY COMMUNITIES
Portland, Oregon
503.221.6911
www.hfhcp.org

WHOLE HOUSE SALVAGE
Palo Alto, California
650.328.8131
www.driftwoodsalvage.com

FRAMING

SIDING &

SHEATHING

Of the approximately 1.5 million new homes built each year in the United States, 90 percent are framed in wood.[1] At a conservative estimate of 400 studs per house, upwards of half a billion studs are required annually for residential construction—not to mention sheathing, flooring, roofing, trim, and cabinetry. But even after a century of continual refinement, stick framing, while swift and convenient, can be a materially inefficient building system. According to Tracy Mumma and Steve Loken of the Center for Resourceful Building Technology, enough studs are wasted on twenty typical job sites to frame an additional house.[2] Despite this staggering volume of materials and waste, many professionals believe that stick framing remains our most practical and efficient way to build. Toward this end, efforts have been underway for decades to streamline engineering, optimize wood use, and minimize construction site waste.

Still others argue that stick framing's dominance should be diminished. Studies at the Fox Maple School of Traditional Building in Brownfield, Maine, suggest, for example, that traditional timber frame construction can save at least 30 percent of the materials used in a comparably sized stick frame building, using logs with shorter maturation cycles in the forest.[3] Green building activist David Eisenberg has even argued that wood should be reconsidered altogether. "If wood were being introduced today it wouldn't have a chance to be accepted by the building codes," he says.[4] Eisenberg, founder of the Development Center for Appropriate Technology in Tucson, Arizona, is a self-proclaimed "recovering contractor" who works doggedly to educate building code officials about the long-term social and environmental impacts of the global construction industry. "Wood is an unstable material with extreme species variability, different strengths and drying requirements. It rots, burns, and is susceptible to bacterial and fungal growth. Even with one or two of these drawbacks, wood couldn't pass the present code requirements, and it has *all* these problems."

Because of the cumulative effects of overharvesting, many builders are choosing to revive and update more traditional systems, emphasizing vernacular designs, regional sources of materials, and site-specific climate considerations. Rather than the conventional residential building process, which relies on an intensive layering of processed industrial materials, there are a number of alternative approaches that offer integrated building systems in which the structural elements are also the finish elements. Rammed earth, adobe, and cob, for example, provide both structural support and finished wall surfaces. Structural posts, beams, rafters and collar ties are often left exposed to add warmth and architectural interest to spaces. Other industrially manufactured building systems have emerged over the past two decades—such as steel framing, structural insulated panels, and insulated concrete forms—that can significantly reduce or eliminate wood from the building frame.

OPTIMUM VALUE ENGINEERING/ ADVANCED FRAMING

Benefits: With proper up-front design, engineering efficiencies can reduce the amount of wood in a building's shell. Double top plates can be eliminated by aligning framing members vertically throughout the structure. Significant cost savings due to material reduction and less waste disposal without sacrificing structural integrity. Works within standards of stick-frame industry—no specialized skills or techniques are required. Thermal bridging can be reduced with advanced framing, resulting in a more energy-efficient building. FSC-certified or reclaimed wood can be used in this approach.

Challenges: OVE requires a significant amount of up-front engineering and training of framing crews to achieve material reduction. For that reason, it is perhaps most appropriate for contractors who can take advantage of economies of scale. Building officials must be consulted early in the process to ensure approval. Because it deviates from conventional spacing practices, there is reluctance by framers to adopt OVE. Sheathing may need to be thicker with increased stud spacing. Check to make sure that siding is appropriate for 24-inch spacing.

Applications: OVE has been used and well documented for some time by numerous organizations, including the National Association of Home Builders Research Center and the Building Science Corporation. An excellent approach for multiple-unit projects but also applicable to single residences. Low-cost housing projects, such as the Casa Verde project in Austin, Texas, have successfully employed OVE techniques.

24 INCHES ON CENTER, 2-STUD CORNERS CAN SAVE MATERIALS, ENERGY, AND MONEY

The National Association of Home Builders Research Center has been promoting a framing materials reduction strategy known as Optimum Value Engineering (OVE) since the 1970s. This approach went largely unrecognized until the 1990s, but since then it is becoming increasingly practiced, and is known both as OVE and 'advanced framing.'

The Massachusetts-based Building Science Corporation has been designing advanced wood framing approaches for decades, saving materials while increasing energy performance. "Wood is the worst possible building system *except*," says architect Betsy Pettit of Building Science Corporation, "except when fairly compared with all other alternative options." Pettit has designed and provided drawings for hundreds of advanced framed structures utilizing a single top plate, two-stud corners, and studs placed at 24 inches on center (16 inches is standard). "Low-tech, labor-intensive building systems may be more appropriate for developing countries where human power is a lot less expensive. But in North America labor remains our most valuable item in the building specs, and the residential construction industry revolves around highly skilled carpenters and highly developed wood-based manufacturing. All of our studies have shown that wood creates the best building envelope using the least embodied, operating, and decommissioning energy overall of any building system."

Architect Ann Edminster, author of the Natural Resources Defense Council (NRDC) book *Efficient Wood Use in Residential Construction*, outlines some of the basic strategies in OVE and advanced framing as follows:

- designing and engineering for materials efficiency (e.g. basing the design on two-foot modules);
- framing at 24 inches on center;
- using two-stud corners and drywall clips to prevent cracking;
- aligning framing and using a single (rather than double) top plate;
- designing headers for loading conditions;
- choosing a slab floor;
- aligning openings with stud spacing.

Increasing stud size from 2x4 to 2x6 and the spacing between studs from 16 to 24 inches is one of the key strategies of advanced framing. With proper up-front design and engineering, this framing configuration doesn't compromise a building's structural integrity. It doesn't require additional materials, and in fact has been shown to significantly reduce jobsite waste. Savings particularly accrue on mass production projects, where labor and material costs can drop as much as a few hundred dollars per house after the initial learning curve has been surmounted.

Advanced framing also improves the opportunity for insulation. Using fewer studs decreases thermal bridging and makes more room for insulation, resulting in a more energy-efficient house. "A 2x6, 24 inches on center, wall system offers higher quality," says Pettit. "For the cost of a few hundred dollars for two extra inches of insulation, the house's thermal performance increases by 50 percent," (and often allows equal or greater savings in the mechanical system).

Throughout many forested areas of North America, wood remains an obvious choice as a regional and vernacular framing system, as long as forestry practices change to make it not only a renewable but an ecologically sustainable resource. There are some challenges, however, particularly in wet and humid regions such as the Pacific Northwest and the Southeast. Changes in building practices, largely driven by more stringent energy codes, are the apparent culprits in a recent increase in structural failures of wood-framed houses. It appears that increasing the thermal insulation of structures (as well as a number of other complex factors), while enhancing energy performance, is also responsible for reducing their longevity by inducing wood rot. A pressing question is how to build more forgiving structures that can experience high levels of moisture without compromising durability. One of the key strategies currently in place involves eliminating vapor barriers on houses in moist climates, creating more permeable or breathable wall systems, along with well-designed moisture shedding exteriors.

The Emeryville ReSourceful Building Project Experience:

- *Roof trusses saved $3,424 or $1.07 per square foot.*
- *Modified OVE designs saved $1,407 or $0.45 per square foot and reduced the wood used in the walls by 19 percent, saving 2,800 board feet of lumber. FSC-certified wood was used for wall framing*
- *Although the certified lumber cost $329 more than conventional framing materials, the overall savings from OVE and trusses totaled more than $4,800.*

Source: Emeryville ReSourceful Building Project, Siegel & Strain Architects.

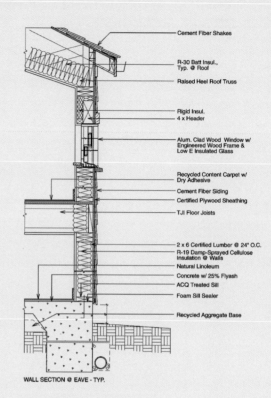

Cement Fiber Shakes
R-30 Batt Insul., Typ. @ Roof
Raised Heel Roof Truss
Rigid Insul.
4 x Header
Alum. Clad Wood Window w/ Engineered Wood Frame & Low E Insulated Glass
Recycled Content Carpet w/ Dry Adhesive
Cement Fiber Siding
Certified Plywood Sheathing
TJI Floor Joists
2 x 6 Certified Lumber @ 24" O.C.
R-19 Damp-Sprayed Cellulose Insulation @ Walls
Natural Linoleum
Concrete w/ 25% Flyash
ACQ Treated Sill
Foam Sill Sealer
Recycled Aggregate Base

WALL SECTION @ EAVE - TYP.

A few design features:

- *Eco-profiles and modified life cycle analyses were done on most of the major design considerations to quantify savings, environmental benefits, and affordability.*
- *An optimized framing system saved 20 percent of the materials necessary.*
- *All framing and finish lumber specified was FSC-certified and readily available from a local supplier.*
- *A mix of 25 percent fly ash was blended into the concrete foundation, requiring less of CO_2-producing Portland cement.*
- *ACQ-treated lumber replaced highly toxic conventional pressure-treated wood (see page 109).*
- *Recycled glass tiles were installed on countertops.*

THE EMERYVILLE RESOURCEFUL BUILDING PROJECT

An affordable housing development in Emeryville, California, a dense residential and industrial city sandwiched between Berkeley and Oakland, is the site of an instructive green building initiative spearheaded by Siegel & Strain Architects. An 'infill' project, this housing complex was designed specifically to blend in seamlessly with the existing residential fabric. Now known as the Emeryville reSourceful Building Project, it became a model on a variety of levels as it applied principles of green building to affordable housing, to quantify environmental impacts and cost differences between standard construction and alternatives, and to arrive at options that were economical and effective. The project consists of three, two-story residential units and totals 5,500 square-feet of living space.

Using the advanced framing techniques developed by the National Association of Home Builders Research Center, Siegel & Strain decided to frame walls at 24 inches on center instead of at the conventional 16-inch spacing. This, they believed, could minimize the amount of framing wood necessary and save money without compromising the structural integrity of the housing units. Their engineer then designed a framing system using the 24-inch spacing for walls, roof, and floor assemblies.

"We actually used a modified version of OVE framing," explained Larry Strain, "keeping 3-stud corners, a double top plate, and using standard trusses 24 inches on center for the roof assembly. Our contractor was suspicious of our 24-inch-on-center stud spacing at first, thinking we were trying to cheat the client out of a stronger building. But as we have learned on a variety of green projects, the architect often has to provide a lot of additional support to the contractor when using new or unusual materials and methods of construction."

Not only was Siegel & Strain able to save approximately 20 percent of the framing lumber, they also specified FSC-certified wood and sheathing throughout the project, including studs, structural plywood, and fencing and trellis materials. 'Eco profiles' and modified life cycle analyses were conducted on most of the major design elements to quantify savings, environmental benefits, and affordability. Alkaline-copper-quaternine (ACQ)-treated lumber replaced the more toxic copper arsenate pressure-treated wood. Fiber-cement siding with a 50-year life expectancy and fiber-cement shingles were chosen as long-lasting, no-maintenance alternatives. A mix of 25 percent fly ash was blended into the concrete foundation, requiring less Portland cement. Recycled tiles were used on kitchen countertops, low-VOC carpets were installed, and the R-20 insulation selected was made from recycled newsprint fill. Attractive trellises and fencing, made of FSC-certified redwood supplied by a local distributor of certified and recycled wood products, extended the commitment to the landscape as well.

Benefits: Extremely durable. Insect- and rot-resistant. Dimensionally stable and consistently uniform. Fire-resistant and won't contribute fuel to a blaze. Highly recyclable, with extensive infrastructures to collect and process post-consumer materials. Light-gauge steel's strength-to-weight ratio is an asset when designing for seismic areas. With high recycled content and high recycling rates embodied energy can be reduced.

Challenges: High embodied energy in initial production, though that decreases each time the product is recycled. Mining practices degrade natural habitats. Air, water, and soil pollution occur during processing and mining, although new regulations and Clean Air standards have resulted in significant improvements. 'Thermal bridging' due to steel's high conductivity requires extra (and sometimes costly) insulation. Some people express sensitivity to being surrounded by metal magnetic fields, despite how well the framing is sheathed. 'Ghosting' can occur in areas of high moisture and significant temperature fluctuation. Proper fastening techniques need to be learned in order to prevent squeaky floors, for instance. Finding a constant supply of skilled labor is perhaps the biggest challenge for residential steel framers.

Applications: For both the production and custom home market. Interior partition walls can be steel-framed without thermal bridging concerns. Specify North American steel framing to achieve at least 25 percent recycled content. Limit transportation of materials by choosing the closest supplier. Provide appropriate thermal insulation to cover external wall studs. Study all the options for both light-gauge and red iron framing including resources from the NAHB Research Center, North American Steel Framing Alliance, and Oak Ridge National Laboratory.

FOUR OLD FORDS OR FORTY-FOUR TREES?

Steel framing. Most carpenters won't touch it and many wouldn't know what to do with it if they did. Critics have expressed concerns about steel's high embodied energy, habitat degradation due to mining, toxic emissions during smelting and manufacturing, and 'thermal bridging,' or its ability to conduct heat and cold. Despite these charges, a dedicated group of independent builders, architects, engineers, and manufacturers remain devoted to bringing steel to mainstream residential construction—and they argue that steel offers environmentally preferable attributes. A new saying goes that you can frame a house with four old Fords (or 44 trees), and according to the Washington, D.C.-based North American Steel Framing Alliance, nearly 50,000 homes used steel in wall assemblies in 1999. Steel framing hot spots include: California; Ontario, Canada; Texas; the Gulf Coast states; Arizona; and Hawaii.

A growing number of builders are framing houses with light-gauge steel studs as a direct substitute for wood studs with 16- or 24-inch spacing. ('Light' in the term refers to the thickness of the steel that forms the studs and the fact that they weigh about 30 percent of comparable wood studs.) Light-gauge steel has been most successful in areas such as Hawaii and Ontario, Canada, where market forces and changes in building approaches have made the switch economically competitive. On the island of Oahu, for example, building codes require wood- framed homes to use treated lumber to thwart termite damage, and 60 percent of new housing there is now steel-framed, according to the Hawaii Steel Framing Alliance.

A smaller number of builders use 'red iron' (also called hot rolled structural steel) to create post-and-beam frames that can be infilled with a variety of materials, including rammed earth and straw bales.

Two questions worthy of close examination are: What are steel's advantages, and can it be used to substitute for or complement wood in the building process?

Endless Recyclability?

Advocates promote steel's environmental attributes, such as its virtually endless recyclability; resistance to rot, fire, and insects; and dimensional stability, which can help in creating a tight building envelope. According to Greg Crawford of the Steel Recycling Institute in Pittsburgh, Pennsylvania, on average in the year 2000, North American light-gauge residential building studs contained 35 percent total recycled materials of which 22 percent was post-consumer content. Red iron and rebar factories do far better, averaging 95 percent recycled content (pre-consumer and post-consumer).

All steel is 100 percent recyclable. For this and other reasons, Crawford believes that the criticism of steel's high embodied energy relative to wood and other alternative materials isn't entirely justified. "Because of steel's long life cycle, its potential for endless recycling, and the increasing efficiencies of each new generation of steel mills, the embodied energy should be amortized over the entire life of the material," says Crawford. "Recycling steel takes a quarter of the energy needed to produce virgin materials."

Because there is so much standing stock of recyclable steel in the world today (cars, ships, I-beams in buildings and superstructures, etc.), a recent life-cycle assessment conducted by Scientific Certification Systems (SCS) in Oakland, California, and released in November 2000 by the Steel Recycling Institute argues that it should be viewed as a sustainable resource.[1] Steel processing has become so efficient, and the resource reserve bases of ore and coal in nature are so vast, say the authors of the report, that the depletion of iron resources is approaching zero, qualifying it as a sustainable resource.[2]

Light-Gauge Skeleton

In areas where economic forces have made wood framing more expensive, light-gauge steel is emerging as an alternative. In recent years, many more tools and techniques have been developed to adapt steel framing to mainstream residential construction.

Pliny Fisk and researchers at the Center for Maximum Potential Building Systems (CMPBS) in Austin, Texas, suggest that unless a building made of virgin wood materials reaches the 60- to 70-year mark (and many modern stick-framed houses won't), it will have more of an ecological impact than a steel-framed building that has the potential to endure or to be recycled over that same time period. Gail Vittori, a senior researcher at CMPBS, cautions against sweeping generalities, however. "Every building material has an impact and every building project is unique. There are always varying degrees of better," explains Vittori. "In the case of choosing steel, some primary considerations include the distance between the building site and the mill (which includes transportation) as well as access to high-recycled-content steel."[3]

Another consideration is the effect of warping over time in conventional houses, especially with the diminishing quality of dimensional lumber. Steel studs and beams form a tightly locked, rigid structure. On the other hand, inferior wood has the potential to warp, twist, and shrink over time. Steel has endurance on its side, as well as fewer limitations on the length of structural members.

Concentrated Resource Use

Could intensive steel production somehow be used to reduce the amount of wood required by residential building, and to complement a truly sustainable certified forest industry? In the case of light-gauge steel framing, the SCS/Steel Recycling Institute study has pointed to the sheer amounts of forest land that could be 'retired' by substituting steel studs for wood. The single large-scale mill documented in the study could produce more than two million tons of galvanized steel—enough for 30 percent of home construction needs in the United States. The equivalent amount of woodland required to match that volume of studs is estimated to be at least 20 million acres. The SCS/Steel Recycling Institute study also reports that the physical disruption of habitat associated with steel production, particularly the impact on endangered species and on hydrology, is minimal. In addition, says SCS research scientist Dr. Stan Rhodes, "thanks in large part to the Clean Air Act, steel is no longer a smokestack industry. With the exception of greenhouse gases, which all industries generate, air emissions do not pose human health risks."

Building Momentum

While many green builders dismiss steel as a sustainable material, momentum for the recognition of light-gauge steel framing is slowly building. Innovations such as easy-to-install L-headers, and floor joist systems have been developed that make steel more economically competitive.

Nuts and Bolts

Red iron high-recycled-content steel is being used increasingly in post-and-beam structures with straw-bale infill. Janice Vascott, a Santa Fe-based architect, says that this system can be materially efficient, cost-effective, and easy to install. Red iron structural framing is also being employed by production homebuilders around the country, such as Western Pacific Homes, Steel Classic Homes, and Creative Steel Frame Homes.

'Thermal studs' are in production that feature patterned slots cut out to decrease thermal conduction without sacrificing structural integrity. Coordinated efforts are being made to educate local building officials about the latest innovations in steel framing. A new comprehensive software package is also available that converts architectural plans into light-gauge steel framing specifications, helping builders greatly reduce engineering costs (see page 59).

Interior walls framed with light-gauge steel studs are frequently specified by the Casa Verde Project in Austin, Texas, an exemplary green redevelopment program that involves disadvantaged youths in building and renovation efforts. "One of the conventional tricks we use with light-gauge steel studs," explained Casa Verde building supervisor Rob Winchester, "is to immediately sheetrock one side of the wall frame. This gives the stud wall some rigidity."

Red Iron Posts and Beams

Some architects and builders are turning to heavier-gauge, high-recycled-content red iron as an alternative to recycled wood post-and-beam framing for natural wall systems, such as straw-bale and rammed earth. Janice Vascott, an architect in Santa Fe, New Mexico, for example, has developed a post-and-beam red iron framing system with straw-bale infill walls. The posts are 3-1/2 inches square; the beam is a C-channel with a single 2x4 wooden top plate; all connections are bolted. "The framing process is fast and doesn't require special expertise," says Vascott. "Steel can bear the load with smaller members, it can be prefabricated to greatly reduce waste, and it's cost efficient as well. It's an excellent solution for straw-bale building."

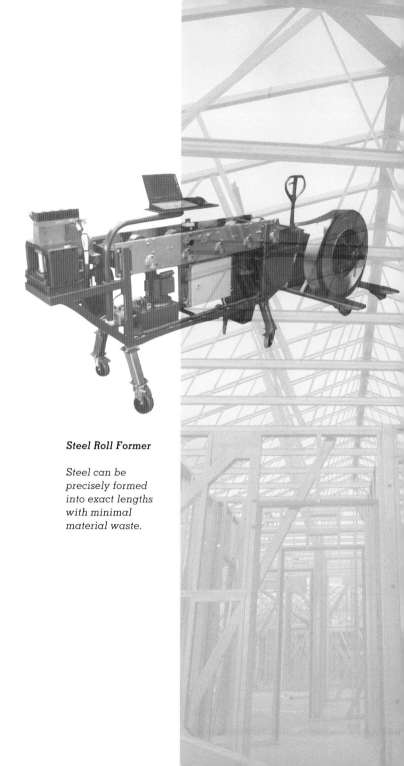

Steel Roll Former

Steel can be precisely formed into exact lengths with minimal material waste.

Production homebuilders throughout the country are framing with red iron as well, and may perhaps be leading the way in using steel to a better advantage. Rather than the stick-for-stick replacement typically used by light-gauge steel framers, bolted red iron framing systems rely on light industrial construction techniques to optimize the load-bearing capacity of heavier steel members, potentially reducing the overall volume of materials. For non-load-bearing walls and floors, light-gauge steel studs are often used. Components are normally prefabricated and shipped as a package for job-site assembly.

Steel's Achilles Heel

More than five years ago, Vermont-based *Environmental Building News* (*EBN*) devoted its entire July/August 1994 issue to the light-gauge steel versus wood framing question. According to author Nadav Malin and the literature available at the time, steel had at least 20 percent more embodied energy than wood (53 million BTUs per ton for steel versus 42 million BTUs for wood, according to one source for a 2,000-square-foot house) and more pollution and toxic emissions related to manufacturing. But it also listed steel's positive attributes, including consistent quality and price stability.

EBN's most compelling argument against steel stud framing focused not on the energy involved in making the stud, but on its thermal performance throughout the life of the building. A highly conductive material, the biggest disadvantage steel posed was thermal bridging—in which cold and heat are conducted by the stud, resulting in undesirable heat loss or gain. Citing a study conducted by the Oak Ridge National Laboratory and reported in the *Journal of Thermal Insulation*, *EBN* reported 16-inch-on-center steel stud construction to have an R-value between 22 and 40 percent lower than comparable wood construction. In cold or hot climates this would seem to make steel prohibitive. However, more than 1,000 houses are being erected in the Toronto area each year—in this climate extensive insulation is required to minimize thermal bridging, whether the framing is wood or steel.

Light-gauge steel framing is typically wrapped in rigid foam insulation to create a thermal break. This can be costly. For interior walls, however, thermal bridging isn't an issue. And in tropical regions such as the Southeast and Hawaii, where wood framing materials are frequently treated with toxic preservatives to ward off rot, diseases, and insect damage (making for heavier and more costly studs), light-gauge steel is increasingly popular.

Reaching for the Max

The Center for Maximum Potential Building Systems in Austin, Texas, (below) is a showcase for regionally sourced and non-wood materials, as well as for designs which emphasize a building's environmental functionality. High-recycled-content steel materials are used in various applications, including columns of rebar and modular framing members.

In many extreme climates, condensation on fasteners passing through insulation can also result in moisture damage. 'Ghosting' is yet another warm climate drawback *EBN* listed, in which electrostatic cling causes dust to collect along the framing; although this can be observed with wood framing as well, repainting is needed more often with steel studs.

In order to put some of these arguments to rest, the Washington, D.C.-based North American Steel Framing Alliance (NASFA) has initiated a series of time and motion studies in three locations—South Dakota, Indiana, and North Carolina—to compare the speed and costs of production, as well as the energy performance over time, of both wood- and steel-framed houses.

A Bright Future?

The challenges of retooling, training skilled labor forces, and economically protecting against thermal bridging have deterred a great many builders, although emerging technical assistance is increasingly addressing these barriers. In countries such as New Zealand, Australia, Switzerland, and Austria, steel framing is firmly established. The future of steel as a mainstream residential alternative to wood in the United States, however, will require creative solutions that take full advantage of steel's strengths, rather than limiting its use to framing practices based on wood. Ensuring that steel's recycled content is maximized is another important goal, as much of its favorable environmental performance relies on this attribute. Market forces will also play a key role, though there are many who predict that changes in climate or other environmental factors may hasten the switch.

Benefits: Can potentially use up to 30 percent less wood. Creates an enduring structural frame that can eventually be recycled. Offers the aesthetic value of exposed wood and fine craftsmanship.

Challenges: Can cost more due to the labor involved in handling, laying out, and joining posts and beams. Can add time to the framing of a building. Infill systems have not been optimized to make timber framing a mainstream product. While organizations exist to support craftsmen, timber framing is a relatively rare skill.

Applications: Timber frame structures are appropriate for residential as well as commercial applications. Timber frame design expertise is essential for maximizing cost effectiveness and in planning for and facilitating future expansion possibilities.

Monastery Masterpiece

The dining hall at the Christ in the Desert Benedictine Monastery, in a remote New Mexico canyon, was designed by Janice Vascott and timber framed by Robert Laporte. The monastery incorporates an inspiring palette of green building approaches: straw-bale, adobe, concrete Trombe walls, timber framing, FSC-certified woods, earthen floors, and solar mechanical systems.

CRAFTING ENDURANCE

Traditional timber framing—the ancient craft of joining large wooden posts and beams to form a durable, beautiful frame for a building—holds great potential to optimize wood use in building. According to author, teacher, and artisan builder Steve Chappell, timber framing with large structural members requires at least 30 percent less material than conventional stick framing. As the square footage increases in a timber frame building, the ratio of timber volume to living area decreases; in a stick-framed structure this ratio of materials to space remains constant. Perhaps most interesting is Chappell's assessment of the timber resources required for the two framing systems. He estimates that producing dimensional lumber for standard framing (2x4s to 2x12s) requires 16-inch logs at a minimum growth cycle of 42 years. Through milling and processing, a considerable amount of that material is lost. Contrary to what one might imagine, Chappell says that the average timber frame house requires relatively few very large timbers. For the 7x10s, 3x8s, 6x8s, and 7x8s, he typically uses logs no more than 14 inches in diameter or much over 37 years old. The majority can be milled from logs less than 10 inches in diameter or from trees less than 27 years old.[1]

While the handling, laying out, and handcrafted joinery certainly is labor-intensive, timber framing does create an enduring structure as well as a visual connection with materials past and present. It has been said, for example, that London's Winchester Cathedral, built in the 1600s, recycled timbers from a building built in the 12th century.[2] As for present reserves of old-growth timber framing materials, a substantial store presently resides in the structures of relict factories and military industrial buildings now being decommissioned all over the country. Timbers also can be obtained from FSC-certified suppliers. New Mexico timber frame artisan Robert Laporte almost always relies on a single forester, whose practices he knows well, for his timbers.

One of the most unfortunate disadvantages of conventional stick framing is that even when skillfully executed with 2x6 FSC-certified lumber, the wood members are soon covered up by both exterior siding and interior paneling surfaces. As mentioned earlier, those studs can become vulnerable to rot if moisture gets trapped within the wall space. Heavy posts and beams, on the other hand, can potentially outlast standard platform framing due in part simply to the size of the members. And when exposed, timbers provide the profound aesthetic values of beautiful wood and fine craftsmanship. In time, a timber structure can also yield materials for reuse in the same way that timbers are now being salvaged and resawn. The same is unlikely to be true for stick framing members.

Every year, 3,000 timber frame houses are built in the United States, a number that is rapidly growing, particularly in the Northeast and Northwest, according to Jerry Rouleau of the Timber Frame Business Council. The majority of those houses presently use structural insulated panels (SIPs, see pages 65–69) to infill the walls, a combination of systems that, while producing an extremely strong building, can create a redundancy and excess of structural materials.

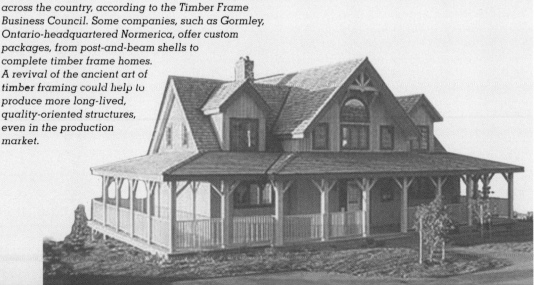

Production Timber Frames

Some 3,000 timber frame homes are built each year across the country, according to the Timber Frame Business Council. Some companies, such as Gormley, Ontario-headquartered Normerica, offer custom packages, from post-and-beam shells to complete timber frame homes. A revival of the ancient art of timber framing could help to produce more long-lived, quality-oriented structures, even in the production market.

While it is typically inadvisable to judge a book by its cover, it is undeniable that a building's exterior wall surfaces are among its most visible and defining features. It is no short order, however, to choose an aesthetically appealing siding material that can stave off years of harsh weather, require minimal repainting or waterproofing, and optimize or substitute for wood. Some traditional building methods, such as rammed earth, create both interior and exterior surfaces along with the basic structure, without the need for additional materials. Most other building systems require a significant amount of siding and sheathing. Fortunately, there are some new choices.

SIDING

North America's most popular siding has traditionally been solid wood, a regionally logical but problematic solution due to decades of overharvesting and the subsequent declining quality of materials. Vinyl siding (made primarily from polyvinyl chloride), long-lasting but often unattractive, is wood siding's chief competitor. PVC is currently under attack by many environmental groups, including Greenpeace, because of the persistent organic pollutants associated with PVC production, and many experts feel it has no place in a healthy structure. It is also difficult to recycle used vinyl siding into other siding products, and this has been rarely done except at the demonstration level. An increasing number of engineered wood paneling products bind either virgin or recovered wood fibers with some kind of formaldehyde-based resin. When using these products, investigate the potential for off-gassing as well as the sources of raw materials.

Another siding solution on the rise is fiber-cement, which blends wood fibers with Portland cement to create low-fuss, 50-year warrantied faux wood siding and roofing materials. Cement-based conventional stucco has provided a durable, low-maintenance siding option for some time, and in certain areas of the country, traditional earth and lime plasters are re-emerging as an exterior finish surface. Metal sidings are high in embodied energy and production impacts, but they are also typically high in recycled content and recyclable. Some metal materials are being selectively integrated in green projects as siding options and even interior wall surfaces.

SOLID WOOD

Solid wood siding products such as bevel lap, ship lap, board-and-batten, and shakes have traditionally come from mature cedar, redwood, and other species that are extremely water- and insect-resistant. The most desirable and durable materials come from old-growth trees—making FSC-certified, recycled, or salvaged materials all viable green options.

On the positive side, wood is renewable, locally available in many regions, relatively low in embodied energy, and ultimately biodegradable. On the other hand, wood siding can require frequent maintenance, generate a fair amount of jobsite waste during construction, and be short-lived.

With the increase in FSC-certified acreage, however, and the intent of large retailers to stock certified building products, there should be an increasing supply of environmentally preferable wood siding options available to builders on a regional basis (see page 38 for a list of websites). FSC-certified composites also should gradually become more available, as the market matures. In Spring 2001, Collins Pine announced the availability of TruWood, an FSC-certified hardboard siding material.

FIBER-CEMENT

Increasing in availability are siding systems in the form of smooth and textural panels, planks, and shingles that combine Portland cement with wood fibers to simulate wood. Green builders are turning to these products because of their relatively low cost and projected longevity. Many have 50-year guarantees, although there are no existing track records to show if they will actually last that long. A significant drawback to fiber-cement is the current sourcing of wood fiber used in some of these products. Apparently, only a handful of species' fibers can tolerate both the hot temperatures generated during processing and the extreme alkalinity of the cement; and those species aren't being harvested on this continent. For example, James Hardie, an Australia-based company and leading supplier of fiber-cement siding, obtains its wood from Australia and New Zealand. Considering the energy-intensiveness of cement manufacture and the overseas transportation of wood fibers (not to mention their uncertified harvesting origins), fiber-cement siding does carry a high embodied energy

burden. Perhaps regional sources of fiber will soon be identified to make this a more resourceful option.

SHEATHING AND WALLBOARD

Among a conventional building's most wood-intensive components are the panels for sheathing exterior walls, floors, and roofs. Since the 1930s, the lion's share of sheathing has been supplied by plywood, although oriented strand board (OSB) has been rapidly gaining since its introduction in the 1980s. For some time, however, a still small but growing diversification away from sole dependence on virgin wood materials for siding and sheathing options has been underway. Today, recycled newsprint, recovered wood waste, byproducts of power incineration (synthetic gypsum), and agricultural fibers are making their way into structural and nonstructural sheathing and other panel products. Some can serve as subfloors and roof decking as well.

STRAW BOARD

Despite a huge production potential across the heartland of North America, the supply of panel board products made from agricultural residues such as straw and sugar cane has been anything but abundant. In late 2000, Mankato, Minnesota-based Phenix Biocomposites introduced a competitively priced, structural strength board made from wheat and soybean straw as a sheathing alternative to plywood and OSB. (See pages 112-115, 118 for more details.) As a board material, straw has some inherent advantages. The microstrands of the fibers reduce the amount of binder necessary for production. Straw boards can also be more water-resistant than wood-based panels.

RECYCLED PAPERS

Each day in northwestern New Jersey, between 150 and 200 tons of newspapers from the surrounding region are turned into sound-deadening acoustical fiberboards, packaging, and other products at the Homasote manufacturing facility. The (non-deinked) newspaper fibers are bound together with a wax emulsion to produce egg carton-like, grey boards in a variety of thicknesses and densities. As a resilient, highly insulative carpet underlayment system, the recycled newsprint board competes with a combination gypcrete and plywood subfloor system. Structural roofing panels from the same materials are also available. Because it has proven remarkably weather-resistant, Homasote board is also being promoted for use as exterior sheathing and is frequently used to fill expansion joints in concrete sidewalks.

For more than 25 years, Simplex Products (now Ludlow Coated Products) in Adrian, Michigan, has been producing thin but remarkably strong panels of 100 percent recycled paper waste (80 percent post-consumer content) that offer superior racking and shear strength. The product literature claims that their structural grade Thermo-ply sheathing can save up to six trees on a standard house. Energy savings are also touted—a building wrapped with the foil-faced boards (with corners overlapped) can produce an extremely tight seal. According to Ann Arbor architect John Barrie, Thermo-ply sheathing has excellent racking strength and is an economical choice for fiber-cement and vinyl-sided homes, among other applications.

Material type/(Product examples)

SOLID WOOD

PLYWOOD

HARDBOARD
(Collins Pine; Masonite; ABTCo; Georgia Pacific; Temple-Inland Forest Products)

OSB

WOOD-RESIN COMPOSITE
(Werzalit; Cladwood)

FIBER-CEMENT
(James Hardie; Maxitile; Cemplank; Certain-Teed; GAF)

STRUCTURAL STRAW BOARD
(Phenix Biocomposites; Pierce Enterprises)

RECYCLED PAPERBOARD
(Homasote; Thermo-ply)

METAL SIDING

SIDING AND SHEATHING OPTIONS

Advantages/Disadvantages	Recommendations
Low energy to manufacture. Renewable and often a local resource. Combustible—may be inadvisable in areas prone to fire. If not old-growth materials, can require frequent maintenance or even replacement.	Specify FSC-certified, reclaimed, and salvaged materials if possible.
Uses more mature wood than OSB or hardboard. Plywood can serve as both siding and sheathing in some cases. Manufacturing pollution can be problematic.	No FSC-certified exterior grade plywood presently available. Optimize material use.
FSC-certified options available. Made from short rotation or immature trees. Potentially a wood-chip product. Some durability problems with certain suppliers. Hardboard often contains less phenol-formaldehyde binder than plywood or OSB.	Specify FSC-certified products. Maximize recycled content and product durability.
Made from short rotation or immature trees. Potentially a wood-chip product. No certified products available. Petrochemical binders required. There have been quality and durability problems in the past.	Look for products with minimal binder. Maximize recycled content and product durability.
Made from sawdust, wood waste, or recycled materials. Uses a synthetic resin binder.	Maximize recycled content and product durability.
Extremely durable, low-maintenance, and fire- and weather-resistant. Many products have low recycled content or imported (non-certified) wood fiber. Can have relatively high embodied energy.	Search for durable products. Look for products with domestic sources of fiber in the future.
Utilizes agricultural byproducts that are often burned. Formaldehyde-free binders used. Limited availability and track record.	Sheathing products only. Look for soy-based resins in the future.
Made from high-recycled-content post-consumer paper waste.	Sheathing, underlayments, and sound boards all available.
Metal products often have a high recycled content but also high embodied energy. Very durable and recyclable.	Check into recycled content and product durability.

Whether building a structure framed with sticks, timbers, or steel, some upfront material sourcing research and planning are highly recommended. FSC-certified (both solid members and engineered products) and salvaged materials can be used in wood-framed structures. Light-gauge steel and red iron framing members should be obtained as locally as possible with the highest recycled content available. Material-saving framing methods such as Optimum Value Engineering initially require a significant investment in research and development, with the maximum benefits accruing through experience. Fortunately there are many excellent resources available, whether you're studying the ancient craft of timber joinery, exploring modern Optimum Value Engineering techniques, or framing with steel. In addition, check into the ever-changing world of sheathing and infill panel products, and determine your siding options in advance to make the most well-rounded decisions possible. For an astonishingly beautiful book on the work of Colombian bamboo-framing architect Simón Vélez, get a copy of Grow Your Own House *(Vitra Design Museum, 2000). Bamboo framing is something that may catch on in some regions of the U.S. in coming decades.*

Optimum Value Engineering Resources

COST-EFFECTIVE HOME BUILDING HANDBOOK and *A BUILDER'S FIELD GUIDE*
800.638.8556/800.223.2665
www.nahbrc.org
The National Association of Home Builders (NAHB) Research Center has been at the forefront of Optimum Value Engineering and these are their resource books on 24-inch framing systems.

EFFICIENT WOOD USE IN RESIDENTIAL CONSTRUCTION: A Practical Guide to Saving Wood, Money, and Forests
Ann Edminster and Sami Yassa
Natural Resources Defense Council (NRDC), 1998.
New York, New York
212.727.2700
www.nrdc.org
An excellent resource for an architect or contractor on ways to optimize wood use in residential construction.

EMERYVILLE RESOURCEFUL BUILDING: ENVIRONMENTALLY SOUND AFFORDABLE HOUSING
Siegel and Strain Architects, 1999.
Available through the Alameda County Waste Management Authority, 510.614.1699
www.stopwaste.org
An inside and comprehensive look at an award-winning low-cost housing project that featured advanced framing and 'eco-profiles' of many non-wood building components.

BUILDER'S GUIDE
Joseph Lstiburek, Building Science Corporation, 1999.
Westford, Massachusetts
978.589.5100

www.buildingscience.com
One of the definitive guides to advanced framing and quality construction detailing. Separate volumes tailored to different climate zones. Updated regularly.

Timber Framing Resources

The website for Acadia Post and Beam and Normerica Building Systems, a commercial supplier of post-and-beam package homes.
www.timberframe.com

MOOSEPRINTS: A Holistic Home Building Guide
Robert Laporte
Econest Building Company
Tesuque, New Mexico
505.989.1813
www.econests.com
A workshop booklet describing the "Econest" building model, including timber frame construction and light straw clay infill walls.

JOINERS' QUARTERLY: The Journal of Timber Framing and Traditional Building
The Fox Maple School of Traditional Building
Brownfield, Maine
207.935.3720
www.foxmaple.com
An outstanding site with great resources, workshop information, and more. This is the site of timber framer and author Steve Chappell, whose recently released *A Timber Framer's Workshop: Joinery, Design and Construction of Traditional Timber Frames* has received very good reviews. Also essential is Chappell's *The Alternative Building Sourcebook*, published by Fox Maple Press.

TIMBER FRAME GUILD
Becket, Massachusetts
888.453.0897
www.tfguild.org
This is an exceptional site, full of information, a workshop calendar, references and resources, including a newsletter, journal, and books. A few recommended titles are *Timber Construction for Builders and Architects* and *Building the Timber Frame House*, by Tedd Benson, as well as the recently released *Build a Classic Timber-Framed House*.

TIMBER FRAME BUSINESS COUNCIL
Hanover, New Hampshire
603.643.5033
www.timberframe.org
A great clearinghouse of information and websites.

Light-Gauge and Red Iron Steel Framing Resources

NORTH AMERICAN STEEL FRAMING ALLIANCE (NASFA)
202.785.2022
www.steelframingalliance.com
Lots of information on steel framing. In particular, see "The National Training Curriculum," an overview of light-gauge steel construction including plans, tools, materials, and complete installation tips.

STEEL FRAME HOUSE CONSTRUCTION
Tim Waite
Craftsman Book Company, 2000
Carlsbad, California
www.craftsman-book.com
New book in tandem with the National Association of Home Builders

STEEL HOME HOTLINE
1.800.79.STEEL
Information on steel building sponsored by the National Association of Home Builders.

LIGHT-GAUGE STEEL ENGINEERING ASSOCIATION
www.lgsea.com
Offers the latest technical standards for light-gauge steel framing primarily for the designer, engineer, architect, or contractor; new details and time-saving tips on installation, including L headers, bridging, connectors, and particularities of steel framing. CD available.
Larry Williams, 615.279.9251
lgsea@aol.com

COMPLETE OWNER-BUILDER SYSTEMS
Santa Fe and Albuquerque, New Mexico
505.989.4400
505.440.5626
Steel framed, straw-bale infill houses pre-designed and delivered to the site.

RED IRON METAL BUILDING MANUFACTURERS ASSOCIATION
www.mbma.com
A website dedicated to red iron construction, primarily for non-residential buildings; plenty of technical information.

STRONG TIE CONNECTORS FOR LIGHT-GAUGE STEEL
Simpson Strong Tie, catalog C-S98
800.999.5099,
Good ideas on connectors for steel framing.

INSULATED STRUCTURAL SYSTEMS

For many decades, builders and companies have been developing complete systems that provide both structure and insulation. A number of these eliminate or substitute for wood and contain recycled materials. Structural insulated panels (SIPs), known also as stressed skin panels, are high-tech sandwiches combining engineered wood sheathing with an insulating inner plank of foam. They can be rapidly erected, and because of their strength and rigidity, they can also reduce the need for some wood compared with conventional stud framing. Straw and other agricultural fibers have been used for compressed agricultural fiber panels for decades in Europe, though North America still lacks a consistent and diverse manufacturing base.

For the present, SIP insulation comes in the form of foam plastics made from petroleum-based chemicals. Foam insulation can and should include materials that have been recycled and/or are produced without ozone-depleting cholorofluo-rocarbons (CFCs) or hydrocholorofluorocarbons (HCFCs). Of the products on the market, expanded polystyrene (EPS) has emerged as the most environmentally preferable type of foam, largely because of its recyclability and its CFC- and HCFC-free processing. While it's impossible to argue that styrofoam puts us on the road toward sustainable building (even if recycling lessens the burden on landfills), foam systems are promoted as 'green' alternatives primarily because they can significantly reduce the operating energy of a building over time.

In addition to thermal performance, foam insulation products have been gaining favor because of their low cost and ease of installation. High-tech foam products sometimes find their way into natural buildings as well, in stem walls, roofs, or as thermal barriers beneath or on the perimeter of earthen floors.

Other recent developments include building block assembly systems that optimize the positive attributes of concrete masonry, but with far better insulating capacity. Over 40 different companies now manufacture and distribute insulating concrete forms, or ICFs, using foam, wood, and other materials to create easy-to-install, high R-value building block systems that can be fortified with rebar and later infilled with concrete to create a monolithic structure. Among the emerging clan of ICFs are a number of noteworthy products that use recycled products or locally available materials to create durable masonry walls or building elements with better performance than conventional concrete.

Concrete, however, perhaps the most ubiquitous human-made material on Earth, ranks among the arch-nemeses of the environmental building movement. Not only have whole mountains been excavated en route to its production, the manufacture of Portland cement, one of its key ingredients, is extremely energy-intensive. According to the American Institute of Architects, 8 percent of global carbon dioxide contributions can be traced to Portland cement manufacture.

At the same time, the extraordinary values of concrete—its thermal mass, ease of installation, relatively low cost, and versatile applications for floors, foundations, stem walls, and bond beams, to name just a few—make it a dependable and almost indispensable construction material, even among natural builders. The National Association of Home Builders reports that the average home uses some 14 tons of concrete. For those and other reasons, efforts have been underway for some time to 'green' concrete by decreasing its Portland cement content and simultaneously boosting its insulation value. Some forms of fly ash—a byproduct of coal fired energy production—can be substituted for cement in the concrete mix. Other products, like recycled foam or wood chips, are being used to augment concrete's meager insulating powers.

The widespread use of fly ash and other similar substitutes can result in a significant reduction of Portland cement consumption around the country. There are various types and millions of tons to be put to the task. Projects at the Austin-based Center for Maximum Potential Building Systems have shown that fly ash can be substituted for as much as 65 percent of the cement in a concrete mix. Such substitutions can also be made for many other building materials containing cement, such as 'PISÉ' (pneumatically impacted stabilized earth, see page 84) and in the concrete structural building systems explained below.

The Sausalito, California-based Ecological Building Network is developing the first comprehensive resource on fly ash and other cement substitutes, to be published sometime in 2001.

Benefits: Could have up to 25 percent recycled core material, though no manufacturer is presently doing so. Wood savings of between 10 and 15 percent are common. Work well as extremely well-insulated roof assemblies. Fast installation. Throughout manufacturing and installation processes, scraps can be used for a variety of applications. Can be prefabricated to precise specifications with limited waste.
Great energy savings.

Challenges: Both expanded polystyrene and polyurethane foam core materials are derived from environmentally hazardous chemicals.
Polyurethane foam can contain HCFCs or other ozone-depleting chemicals through January 1, 2003, when their use has to be phased out.
Plumbing and wiring require advanced planning. Reports vary about the amount of wood actually saved by SIPs. Tighter building shell often necessitates mechanical ventilation.

Applications: Generally regarded as a wood-, money-, and energy-saving approach.
Custom houses often use SIPs for wall or roof systems with all the above benefits.

HIGH-TECH SANDWICH CONSTRUCTION

Imagine building assemblies that virtually snap together in load-bearing, pre-insulated panels, eliminate a significant percentage of the lumber used in stick framing, and reduce the energy required to heat and cool the structure throughout its lifetime. The concept behind structural insulated panels—SIPs—has been around for decades. The structural properties derive from two pieces of high shear-value, oriented strand board (OSB), plywood, or straw board that sandwich a 4-, 6-, or 8-inch slab of polystyrene or polyurethane foam core. Labor- and energy-efficiency are among the principal benefits of this approach. SIPs also offer significant potential for wood savings.

Proponents argue that SIP technology offers a far better use of resources than conventional wood or steel framing systems that also depend upon foam insulation. Once a crew gains experience with SIPs, assembly can be relatively quick, presenting a viable replacement for mass market construction that utilizes the same tools and trades. With the right equipment (i.e., skilled labor and lifting machinery) and setup, floors, walls, and roofs can be erected with little additional structural support. SIPs come in various sizes—from 4 feet by 8 feet to as long as 24 feet—and produce airtight, strong, highly insulated buildings.

David Wright, a Grass Valley, California, solar designer who helped coin the term 'passive solar design,' became interested in SIPs in the late 1980s because of the high R-values the system offers. An architect who works with a variety of natural and green building approaches, he also co-founded a local manufacturing company, Better Building Systems, which fabricates structural insulated panels. "This is a high-tech concept," Wright believes, "that measures up pretty well environmentally. The plywood skins are presently made from plantation alder or poplar using an isoset adhesive, meaning no formaldehyde or urethane is used in the binder." (Incidentally, short-rotation poplar has fiber characteristics very similar to wheat straw.[1]) In addition, Wright sees this system as materially efficient. "By having designs finalized beforehand, we can custom fabricate an exact building envelope, including openings for windows and doors, while minimizing waste at the prefabrication plant. All leftovers from the manufacturing process can be easily recycled." Factory scraps can be ground up and added to road surfaces, for example, and have even been experimented with for potting soil amendments.

"The main issue with the SIP system right now lies in the manufacture of expanded polystyrene or EPS," says Wright. This means that most of the impacts are at the front-end of the manufacturing process. Pentane, used in EPS manufacturing, should be carefully controlled and recycled during manufacture and can even be recaptured for fuel. Once manufactured, the EPS foam, which is also commonly used for such things as disposable coffee cups and flotation devices, remains stable. No off-gassing reportedly occurs over the life of the building. On the other hand, polyurethane will off-gas over time, releasing potentially harmful fumes and reducing the insulation value of the product.

According to *Environmental Building News*, however, both EPS and polyurethane foam used by different manufacturers are derived from toxic and environmentally hazardous chemical intermediaries.[2] *EBN* also reports that with both types of foam, the greatest impacts are not at the plant where SIPs are manufactured, but rather at the chemical factories where the constituent chemicals are initially produced. EPS does not contain HCFCs or other ozone-depleting chemicals, while polyurethane manufacturers can continue using them through January 1, 2003, when their use has to be phased out.

According to the Center for Resourceful Building Technology, although the foam core is a non-renewable resource, it is a relatively efficient use of materials. "One quart of an oil refining byproduct is expanded to create forty quarts of EPS foam."[3] Further, the insulating performance of the material is relatively high, potentially justifying the manufacturing impacts by improving the energy efficiency of the structure throughout its operating life. Wright foresees that "one day in the not too distant future, agricultural crops will be used to manufacture bio-based insulation as an economical option to using petroleum products."

What happens to these panels if a building is disassembled? It depends upon the material in the foam core.

EPS is a 'thermoplastic,' meaning that it can be melted down or ground up and remanufactured into other polystyrene products. Most polyurethane is a 'thermoset' plastic which can only be ground down and not melted, and recyclability is therefore limited. Recyclability, in addition to the ozone issue, is another reason EPS is sometimes seen as environmentally preferable to polyurethane. As stated above, many SIP producers recycle pre-consumer cut-offs throughout the manufacturing cycle, and job site scraps can be used for constructing headers, filler sections above windows, and other creative applications.

Information varies about the amount of wood SIP systems actually save over conventional stick-framed houses. Most SIP designs call for 2x framing at panel joints, around window and door openings, for the top and bottom plates, and at corners. According to a University of Oregon study, a completely panelized house saved 2,720 board feet of wood—or nearly 50 percent of the framing lumber in a conventional house. Wright and other SIP manufacturers contend that lumber reduction can be as high as 40 percent. The Center for Resourceful Building Technology estimates that an average wall section uses 25 percent less wood than its stick-framed equivalent.

"If you're willing to use a calculator you can really save wood," says John Barrie, an Ann Arbor-based architect who regularly specifies SIPs, primarily because of their superior energy performance, and ease of construction. Barrie reports that the load-bearing capacity of SIPs enables him to engineer buildings without headers above windows and doors. He also uses SIP scraps for soffits and is working on insulated lightweight concrete SIPs to replace concrete block walls.

The economic savings for contractors once they get up to speed with SIP technology are more widely acknowledged. Based on data from the University of Oregon study mentioned above, the Natural Resources Defense Council calculated that a builder with ten crews can increase profits by $60,000 annually using stressed skin panels—or a 16 percent boost in yearly profit. The University of Oregon study predicts that as laborers become more familiar with SIPs, the savings become greater still.

In addition to the speed of construction, the overall energy efficiency of the house is enhanced. SIPs have relatively high R-values per inch of thickness and, with

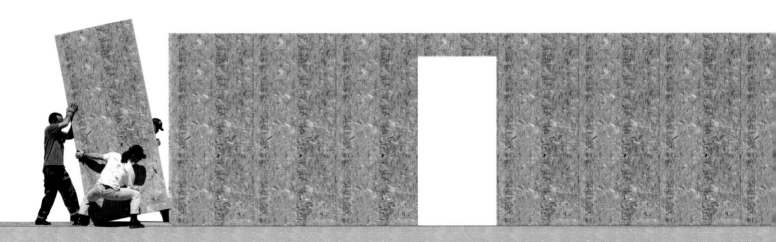

PASSIVE SOLAR RANCH HOUSE

Howard and Mary Lentzner of Brentwood, California chose an SIP system using R-Control panels after learning about passive solar design and later deciding to move back to the family dairy farm and build a new home. The walls went up within two days but then work stalled out quickly when no contractors were available to help with the roof and interior framing. "But our biggest hurdle was the building department," Howard explained. "They weren't used to a building envelope with no framing, and despite our urgings, didn't inspect the project until the walls were up. By that time it was too late to see how the panels were tied down to the foundation since the SIPs include the entire wall assembly." A letter from their engineer was needed to convince the building department about the integrity of the structure. Their project now complete, the Lentzners are very content with the end result, insisting that they "can't see a better way to construct a building."

Howard and Mary offer the following advice to owner-builders interested in SIPs:

- Recruit local people to do the construction work from the beginning.
- During installation, leave an eighth-inch gap between panels while erecting the structure to compensate for the building being off dimensionally in any direction. This gives some flexibility in squaring up the structure to the foundation or slab.
- Design and configure utility systems in advance. Running wires or routing for plumbing through the foam core after the walls have been erected can pose significant challenges. Get shop drawings of the panel system prior to fabrication showing exact electrical and plumbing layouts to eliminate problems. (Most SIPs are now pre-routed for all electrical needs).
- Evaluate the building site. A forklift and crane are usually necessary for unloading and hoisting panels into place.
- Do some homework on the fastening technology, which includes adhesive (it can be expensive) and long screws that can be challenging to install.

proper design, can greatly reduce thermal bridging as compared with stick- or steel-framed houses.

Wright, who not only designs SIP houses but manufactures panels as well, says this type of building system is still in its infancy. What interests him is the applications for SIPs in straw-bale and other thick-walled structures. "SIPs can be used for roofs on straw-bale and adobe structures," he explains. "One of our goals is to make panels with soybeans, straw, or other agricultural residues as the insulator. For the time being, the use of EPS in structural panels is essentially permanent and is a far better use of petroleum than combustion or for drink cups."

Throughout the past few decades, a number of North American companies have attempted to crack the insulated panel market with systems that use straw for insulation, structural skins or both. Pierce Enterprises, an Englewood, Colorado-based manufacturer, was the only U.S. supplier of compressed straw panels at the time this book went to press. Phenix Biocomposites of Mankato, Minnesota began producing structural strand board from agricultural residues at the end of 2000. (These products are described in more detail on pages 112–115, and 118.)

What are some of the downsides to this building approach? Plumbing and electrical work require advance planning, although most manufacturers now incorporate integral routing in their panels. Larger panels, often used for floors and roofs, can be so heavy that cranes are needed for assembly. On remote, small jobs this could be challenging.

Another important consideration is insect control. Ants and termites can nest in the foam. To counter this, some panel manufacturers treat SIPs with borate, a non-toxic, natural fire-retardant that also deters insects. According to Wright, "For the bugs, it's kind of like eating microscopic bits of broken glass. Once they try it, they lose interest very quickly."

Sandwich Construction

There are dozens of suppliers of SIPs systems across the country and a growing cadre of ardent proponents.
See *www.sips.org* for a database.

Benefits: Highly insulating, modular material. Reportedly made from post-consumer recycled styrofoam. Creates durable, thick-walled structures. Easily worked and shaped into free flowing forms. Offers a low-maintenance alternative to adobe.

Challenges: Cutting and rasping on the job site are reported to produce fine dust particles. The recycled content of the material is not verifiable. Cement content is energy intensive. At present, transportation is a critical issue.

Applications: Can be used for entire load-bearing building systems as well as stem walls and foundations. Many creative uses for scrap materials. Earth plasters adhere well to wall surfaces. Extremely popular in southwestern states which are near the source of manufacture (in Mexicali, and Juarez, Mexico). Similar plants are expected to be opened in the United States in the near future.

RECYCLED STYROFOAM PACKAGE DEAL

Its name sounds Jamaican, it looks like giant Rice Krispy biscuits, and it's partially derived from the stiff foam packaging forms used to ship computers, televisions, and other consumer goods. In the words of Austin architect and builder Marly Porter, "Rastra is adobe that doesn't fall apart." The product has made its appearance across the United States in different regions over the last decade (with particular success in the Southwest). Similar products have been used in Europe for decades, where concrete and masonry construction are the norm rather than the exception.

The Rastra system is somewhat unique among ICFs in that it is made primarily from recovered polystyrene packaging, which is ground up into BB-like beads, mixed in a slurry containing about 15 percent cement (by volume), and cast into interlocking building blocks. The cement serves as a binding agent, individually coating and holding all those tiny beads together, creating both fire and water resistance. The blocks are typically 10 feet long, 10 inches wide, and 15 or 30 inches high, weigh about 150 pounds each, and are stacked and then glued in place. After the blocks are glued, the walls can be shaped, rounded, contoured, and sandblasted. Holes, or cores, approximately 4 inches in diameter are pre-cast into the Rastra blocks at 15 inch intervals. In addition, there are semi-circular channels where each block adjoins the one above or below it. This network of cores and channels produces a grid into which rebar can be inserted every 15 inches on center, both vertically and horizontally. Concrete is then poured into the holes, infilling the blocks and creating an extremely heavy, monolithic fortress of a structure. After that foam-rebar-concrete wall system is completed, stucco and plaster (including beautiful earthen and lime plasters) are typically applied to the exterior and interior of the building.

Rastra is a particularly appropriate choice for builders in the Southwest, who are close to the manufacturing facilities in Mexico. In addition to whole house systems, it is frequently used for stem walls and foundations (especially where radiant floors are installed) and where structures are built into the ground.

There are a number of environmental drawbacks to the product. First is the energy-intensive nature of the manufacture of both the cement and the expanded polystyrene. Next is the adhesive used to glue the blocks together. Some of the applicator containers use an hydrocholorofluorocarbon (HCFC) ozone-depleting propellant. Finally, it's been hard both to verify the recycled content of the Rastra product and to pin down the actual R-value, although the homeowners we've talked to are satisfied with the thermal performance of the system.

There are some other bright sides, including durability, disaster resistance, and energy performance. Because each foam bead is coated with cement slurry, it is unlikely that Rastra will be susceptible to insect infestations, a concern frequently raised about foam building systems. In addition, this technology can potentially be applied on a 'mini-mill' basis, utilizing waste materials economically within a 500-mile radius to supply a local area with building systems. At least one pilot plant for a similar product named MonolithWalls is expected to be up and running in the U.S. sometime in 2002.

RECOMMENDATIONS FROM A FEW RASTRA USERS

- *Have at least one person who has experience working with Rastra on your team.*
- *Access to the site is important. The material is shipped on 48-foot trailers, and a forklift is helpful to move materials around.*
- *A relatively flat staging ground makes it easier to manage and work with materials.*
- *Rastra blocks are heavy, about 150 pounds each, requiring workers in good physical condition.*
- *Don't start a job during the rainy season; keep blocks covered and off the ground at all times.*
- *Keep designs simple. Consider a slab-on-grade rather than a raised floor.*
- *Concrete can 'blow out' while pouring the forms. Watch out for corner joints, window joints, and other places where concrete might break through. Use end elements, provided by supplier for corners and windows, or reinforce vulnerable places with concrete ties. Also, insist that concrete pourers go slowly and move back and forth carefully across the structure to give concrete time to settle.*
- *Specify at least 15 percent of fly ash in the concrete formula to reduce Portland cement content.*
- *Use leftover pieces creatively, to build landscape walls, foundations, outbuildings, or headers.*
- *Design in a mechanical ventilation system to provide adequate air exchange.*
- *Seal interior panel joints with quality construction tape.*

Rastra Rendering

This architectural rendering by Craig Henritzy shows a residence nestling within the contours of the landscape.

Recycled Block Fence

Only now are Rastra's limits really being tested. Leftover pieces can be used in a variety of applications. Outside Marly Porter's studio in Austin, Texas, is a fence made from leftover scraps, with a decorative pattern removed from the otherwise solid-surface material.

Pueblo Details

Rastra is well-suited to the architectural styles of the Southwest. Taos-based solar designer Karlis Viceps has been using Rastra in pueblo-style and passive solar homes like this for many years with great satisfaction. The photo, second from the bottom, details a pre-manufactured roof truss joining the wall. At bottom left is a column base just completed.

RECYCLED WOOD/CONCRETE BLOCK SYSTEMS

Benefits: Can be sawn, nailed, glued, and worked with standard carpenters' tools. Purportedly utilizes wood from the waste stream, and agricultural fibers and residues can be used as well. Resists rot and moisture. More breathable than conventional masonry. Potential for mini-mill production in some regions of the country. One product uses three percent fly ash in place of cement. More energy-efficient than concrete block. Can withstand severe storms and hurricanes.

Challenges: Limited distribution, although these products are gaining increasing use throughout the country. The sources of raw materials are not verifiable. Concrete masonry is an energy-intensive material.

Applications: Foundations, stem walls, or entire masonry buildings. Blocks are dry stacked, set internally with a grid of rebar, then filled with concrete, creating an interlocking post-and-beam effect. Various interior and exterior surfaces can be applied. Wiring can be run through cores in grooves routed out on the block face.

WOOD WASTE MASONRY

Praised by many natural builders as the premiere 'green' insulated concrete form, Faswall was developed by Swiss architect Hans Walter in the late 1980s in response to what he considered shoddy American building standards, particularly in the Southeast, which is prone to frequent hurricanes and tornadoes. The patented formula for Faswall blocks consists of ground-up wood waste coated in clay and then mixed in a slurry containing 12 percent Portland cement and 3 percent fly ash. With a reported R-value of 18, the blocks are well-suited for many applications.

While a similar technology has been used in Europe for decades, Hans Walter and his wife Leni developed a process to utilize discarded pallets and other locally sourced wood waste, rather than the traditional virgin spruce. Originally, European builders mixed straw and clay. This approach later evolved into a wood-concrete wall form system after World War II. In the Faswall system, the clay coating closes the wood pores and allows the cement to perform as a bonding agent. According to Leni Walter, agricultural fibers such as rice straw, rice hulls, and other crop residues can be substituted with equally positive results.

In addition to high accolades for performance, perhaps the most encouraging thing about the Faswall system is its mini-mill potential. If located within reasonable distance of a ready source of fibers—right now the Arkansas-based plant takes advantage of the Mississippi River transportation system—a plant can be set up for under $2 million to process up to 50,000 tons of wood waste (or agricultural fibers) per year.

Ontario, Canada-based manufacturer, Durisol, also supplies recycled wood and concrete blocks to builders across North America. Durisol's blocks utilize post-industrial manufacturing scrap and contain no fly ash. These blocks are used in high-rise buildings as well as in single family homes. In addition to blocks, the company offers retaining wall and noise barrier systems.

Putting Up Walls Against Waste

According to Faswall developer Hans Walter, 1.6 million tons of wood waste could produce enough Faswall blocks to make 300,000 1,800-square-foot homes. He estimates that's less than one-third of the wood waste presently burned or landfilled each year in the U.S.
Source: Concrete Products, January 2000.

ECO-CRETES

Another lightweight, insulating masonry system gaining in popularity in some areas of the United States is autoclaved aerated concrete (AAC) a.k.a. autoclaved cellular concrete (ACC). AAC systems come in blocks or panels, have excellent thermal performance characteristics, and are as durable and workable as lumber. The steam-curing manufacturing technique they utilize originated in Europe some 80 years ago, and various products are now on the market, under such names as Ytong, Hebel, Contec, and LiteBuilt. While reportedly on the expensive side, these systems fully merit consideration and investigation.

Pumicecrete, another "eco-crete" alternative, relies upon the waste product of regional volcanic rock mining—pumice—to create a well-insulated masonry wall system. "What I like most about pumicecrete is its simplicity," says Scott McCarty, a masonry contractor who works primarily with pumicecrete throughout New Mexico and other southwestern states. "It's a low-density concrete that is ten parts pumice, one part cement and water."

A highly sculptural medium, pumicecrete is usually poured in place into reusable forms to create monolithic wall systems. The pea-gravel-sized pumice stones trap air within the wall to create a system that insulates better than concrete. It's economically competitive as well. "I've produced more than a few pumicecrete homes for single moms with FHA loans," McCarty says.

Mining pumice for stonewashing textiles has been the subject of considerable outrage in the Southwest—particularly when it has occurred in sacred Native American sites— but McCarty argues that it is an efficient use of resources and that mining operations have improved significantly.

Pumicecrete construction is only an option where the material occurs naturally. It is found in parts of New Mexico, Arizona, California, Oregon, Washington and Idaho, according to the Center for Resourceful Building Technology. Other types of volcanic rock occur in Hawaii.

RESOURCES

While insulating structural systems offer many potential benefits, there are still some outstanding concerns about the sources of raw materials used. Whenever possible, question suppliers about the sources of these products. Green building publications, such as *Environmental Building News* (www.buildinggreen.com) and *Environmental Design and Construction* (www.edcmag.com), offer regular in-depth features on insulating concrete forms and structural insulated panels. Gaining insight from builders who have experience working with these systems can greatly help with project planning. With any luck, and consumer pressure, these types of modular structural products will increasingly become regionalized and take advantage of the insulating powers of waste foam or agricultural residues.

Structural Insulated Panels

THE STRUCTURAL INSULATED PANEL ASSOCIATION (SIPA)
Washington, DC
202.347.7800
www.sips.org
Excellent resource materials on building with SIPS.

BUILDING WITH STRUCTURAL INSULATED PANELS
Michael Morley
www.sips.org
A highly recommended new text offering an overview and practical how-to details of building with SIPs.

UNIVERSITY OF OREGON CENTER FOR HOUSING INNOVATION
Department of Architecture
Eugene, Oregon
541.346.3656
Has conducted numerous tests and developed their own models for building with stressed skin panels. Publications available.

EFFICIENT WOOD USE IN RESIDENTIAL CONSTRUCTION: A Practical Guide to Saving Wood, Money, and Forests
Ann Edminster and Sami Yassa
Natural Resources Defense Council (NRDC)
New York, New York
212.727.2700
www.nrdc.org
An excellent resource for an architect or contractor on ways to optimize wood use in residential construction, with a specific chapter on SIPs.

CENTER FOR RESOURCEFUL BUILDING TECHNOLOGY
Missoula, Montana
406.549.7678
www.crbt.org

ENVIRONMENTAL BUILDING NEWS
Brattleboro, Vermont
802.257.7300
www.buildinggreen.com

Structural Straw Panels

PIERCE ENTERPRISES, INC.
Englewood, Colorado
800.297.6955
Wall and floor panels made from waste straw.

PYRAMOD INDUSTRIES INTERNATIONAL
Grass Valley, California
530.742.1846
Straw panel manufacturing systems.

Selected Architects and Information about SIPs

DAVID WRIGHT ASSOCIATES, AIA-Environmental Architects,
Grass Valley, California
530.477.8017
www.dwrightaia.com
SIPs designer, manufacturer and green architect.

JOHN BARRIE ASSOCIATES ARCHITECTS
Ann Arbor, Michigan
734.668.4811
Green architect working on a concrete SIP.

Fly Ash Information Centers

ECOLOGICAL BUILDING NETWORK
Sausalito, California
415.331.7630
www.ecobuildnetwork.org
Upcoming resource guide on cement replacements, including fly ash, and other leading-edge research and consulting.

CENTER FOR MAXIMUM POTENTIAL BUILDING SYSTEMS
Austin, Texas
512.928.4786
www.cmpbs.org
Pioneering work on the use of fly ash.

Selected Insulating Concrete Form suppliers

ICF Web
www.icfweb.com
Includes a product guide and directory as well as a how-to section on selecting a contractor, news, project information and more.

FASWALL
K-X Industries
Windsor, South Carolina
800.491.7891
www.faswall.com

DURISOL
Hamilton, Ontario, Canada
905.521.0999
www.durisol.com

PUMICE-CRETE BUILDING SYSTEMS of New Mexico
El Prado, New Mexico
505.751.3076
www.pumicecrete.com

A Return to Traditional and Vernacular Construction   At the vanguard of green construction is the natural building movement. Multifarious in its inspiration—the allure of thick-walled structures and natural materials; the owner-builder ethic and the urge for self-sufficiency; the turn away from globally sourced, energy-intensive, conventional building elements—this movement has been growing for decades. Natural building is perhaps best exemplified by straw-bale and various forms of earthen construction. The movement's emphasis is on using, as much as possible, locally available and relatively unprocessed materials such as clay excavated from a building site, stone hauled from a nearby source, timbers milled from an adjacent woodlot, or straw-bales purchased from a regional farmer. Natural buildings also often take advantage of solar energy for passive heating and cooling.

Thanks to the work of pioneers in the natural building movement, perceptions about appropriate construction technologies are slowly changing. Straw-bale, rammed earth, cob, and adobe buildings, timber framing, light straw clay, and earth-based plasters, paints and floors, are just a few of the many methods and materials being used across North America today, re-entering the building vocabulary and even appearing in local and regional building codes.

The challenge of the natural building movement has been and remains to adapt traditional and vernacular building approaches to today's standards for performance, comfort, durability, safety, and even perhaps, population density. Like the organic farming movement, natural building has been characterized by a strong sense of camaraderie and an open sharing of information. Each successive project seems to take on some new challenge, trying to raise the bar just a little higher in an attempt to improve the quality and utility of these construction techniques. As any builder, architect, or engineer will no doubt caution, however, the amount of expertise required to produce a great green building should not be underestimated. The natural building movement, then—like the conventional building industry—has its share of failures built by amateurs limited by their own skill and knowledge. The basics of good roofs and overhangs, adequate foundations, and good moisture control strategies are nearly universal to the success of natural buildings. For roofs and foundations in particular, natural builders are apt to choose manufactured materials, in a trade-off to create a long-lived, low-maintenance structure.

Part of the attraction of natural building lies in its low-tech methods and artisanal aesthetic. Natural building projects also frequently feature traditional barn raisings, community work parties, or on-site workshops.

Conventional stick building can be described as a process of layering, with a series of materials applied to the skeletal frame, leaving flat, painted surfaces exposed in the end. In contrast, most natural building techniques—log buildings, timber framing, cob—are whole systems in that the structural elements are also the finish elements. This quality of craftmanship and the touch of the human hand makes natural building appeal to many people with its rounded, uneven wall surfaces, windowsill embrasures wide enough to lounge in, the leathery softness of an earthen floor under bare feet, or the raw character of rough-sawn timbers.

Natural builders are to the construction industry what Biodynamic and small-scale organic farmers are to the sustainable agriculture movement. They are shifting the process of green building to a local level and developing techniques, models, and materials, some of which will someday make their way into the mainstream through hybrid designs and light-industrial-scale applications. Already, straw-bale construction has been carried out in multi-unit housing developments, as has compressed soil block building. Seminars are being held somewhere in the country nearly every week to offer hands-on experience in one or more natural building methods.

While natural building's market share will probably remain just a fraction of the construction industry, the movement's objectives and obvious advantages have already begun to influence the broader culture. Natural building has already helped to emphasize the importance of regional, vernacular approaches to solving our needs for shelter. The degree to which these traditional approaches and materials are married with new technologies, building codes, contractors, and materials distributors will ultimately determine whether the average homeowner will benefit from their excellent advantages such as low toxicity, energy efficiency, opportunity for owner involvement, and local resourcefulness.

Janice Vascott, of Santa Fe, New Mexico, is one architect who has begun to combine a variety of different wall system materials based on their individual attributes. In her design for the Christ in the Desert Monastery north of Abiquiu,

New Mexico, Vascott used three different wall materials to achieve her passive solar goals. A south-facing concrete thermal mass wall was combined with adobe interior walls for added thermal mass, and straw-bale walls for insulation on the north, east and west—using each material to its particular advantage.

Perhaps the natural building movement's most unsung contribution is the diplomatic work now underway helping to empower local communities in developing countries. While people around the world are wanting to raise their living standards by creating modern industrial houses, pioneers such as Nader Khalili, Bill and Athena Steen, Kelly Lerner, Steve MacDonald, Matts Myhrman, Alfred von Bachmayr, Steve Kemble, Carol Escott, Frank Meyer, and many, many others are working to teach people the benefits and qualities of technologically appropriate, locally oriented, low-cost, natural building methods.

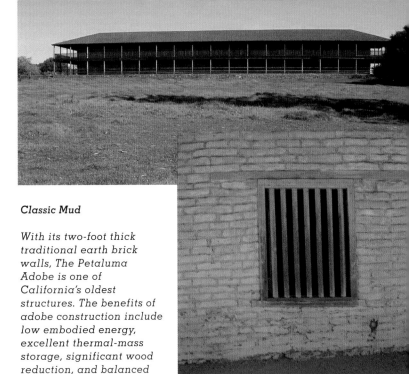

Classic Mud

With its two-foot thick traditional earth brick walls, The Petaluma Adobe is one of California's oldest structures. The benefits of adobe construction include low embodied energy, excellent thermal-mass storage, significant wood reduction, and balanced indoor air quality.

Native Condo

The Taos Pueblo, an earthen apartment complex, is the country's oldest continuously lived-in structure. It is also a testament to the endurance of vernacular earth building techniques and passive solar design in multi-story applications. Native American peoples evolved their own methods from previous multi-story structures on the cliffs and mesas of the canyonlands.

Benefits: Creates a market for agricultural waste product. Excellent insulation value. Energy-efficient, extremely quiet, natural aesthetic. Can be inexpensive as an owner-builder option, though contractor-built straw-bale homes are generally more expensive. Straw bales could be certified organic. Labor-intensive but high potential for owner involvement and volunteer work parties. Straw-bale is the least expensive of thick-walled construction methods, primarily because of the speed with which walls can be built.

Challenges: Bales, like all wood-based products, must be kept dry before and after installation. Further testing is needed for widespread acceptance in certain areas of the country. If contractor-built, in certain areas can be more costly than conventional building. Careful weatherproofing is important.

Applications: Simple designs that factor in the limitations and dimensions of the bale will be most cost-effective. From gardening sheds to custom houses to public libraries, especially appropriate where high levels of thermal and acoustic insulation are desired.

GOOD SHOES, A GOOD HAT, AND A COAT THAT BREATHES

Practiced for centuries in Europe and Asia in various forms, building with straw began in the United States, according to most sources, in the Sandhill region of western Nebraska in the late 1880s. The invention of the steam-powered baler, combined with the region's dearth of timber and stone, sparked this innovation in building assembly. Many straw-bale structures built in the area between 1880 and 1930 exist today in remarkably sound condition. In fact, 'Nebraska style' refers to the load-bearing construction technique common in that region, in which the straw bales not only produced well-insulated, two-foot-thick walls, but also supported the weight of roof and floors.

A grassroots (no pun intended) straw-bale building revival began in the 1970s, primarily in the arid southwestern United States and mainly among people looking for affordable do-it-yourself building approaches. Passive solar benefits and the comforting quiet of bale-wide walls were equally appealing.

Anyone who has ever spent any time in one of these thick-walled, well-insulated structures can easily understand the draw of straw-bale. There is something undeniably charming about the rounded, non-uniform plastered surfaces, about the opportunity to lounge inside a windowsill full of cascading sunlight. But the real benefits take place on the landscape. In the early 1990s, a growing awareness of the millions of tons of straw that were either burned or left to rot in fields across Canada and the United States sent people scrambling for new products and outlets to utilize those fibers—not just for buildings, but paper, packaging, and other wood-based industrial products. Poor air quality was also epidemic in agricultural regions of the country where annual post-harvest straw burning had reached unhealthy levels. Combined with the ever-increasing pressures on forests for fibers, the idea of utilizing agricultural 'waste' straw, captured the imagination of a new generation.

By the mid-1990s, hundreds of straw-bale structures had been erected in North America and abroad, and not just by owner-builders but also by skilled contractors serving the high-end custom home market. As a result, a wide range of physical examples of straw-bale buildings now exists by which to assess the technology. Early pioneers have had the dubious honor of being the front-line troops with building departments that have not always been receptive. These early efforts have also laid the framework for engineering and testing necessary to create long-lived structures, as well as providing performance data covering a broad spectrum of climatic and seismic conditions under which straw-bale has to perform.

According to David Arkin, a California straw-bale pioneer and principal of Arkin Tilt Architects in Berkeley, "There are three golden rules for turning straw into a great building. Good shoes—a proper separation between the foundation and bale walls. A good hat—generous overhangs that keep moisture away. And a coat that breathes—a vapor- permeable stucco or lime plaster skin."

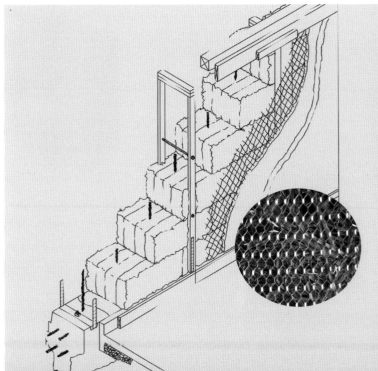

Raising Bales

While volunteers are often recruited to join the 'bale raising,' the load-bearing systems are carefully detailed and constructed. Both load-bearing and non-load-bearing (a.k.a. post-and-beam) systems are in continual evolution. This diagram shows bales stacked in a running bond like bricks, with internal pins. Pinning adds structural stability and bracing until plaster skins and the roof structure are in place. Internal pinning is now giving way to methods that place structural rebar on either side of the bale, wired together at each row of bales, or in the case of some post-and-beam systems, no pinning at all. Stucco wire is frequently secured to the bales and the structural framing members, enhancing stability. (Diagram: Arkin Tilt Architects, Albany, California.)

These fundamental rules deal primarily with preventing the straw bales from decomposing, due to either water penetration from the exterior or accumulation of moisture from interior sources (such as cooking, showering, respiration, etc). After all, straw bales are biodegradable, not unlike wood, their more conventional cousin. Some straw-bale walls have had to be torn apart because moist bales were set in place, plastered, and later began to rot. In addition to preventing moisture from collecting inside the walls, a well-thought out interface between bales and the foundation can prevent disaster. Without such foresight and proper design, a flood, for example—even one caused by an obstructed washing machine—can damage the bales. Generous roof overhangs shelter the walls from all but the most fiercely wind-driven rain.

These important issues aside, a great deal of the beauty of this wall building method rests with the opportunities for owners and volunteers to participate in bale-raising. Tools are fairly simple, ranging from utility knives to weed-eaters to chain saws. The bales are stacked like oversized bricks and are then either spiked together (a method currently falling out of favor) or caged with rebar, bamboo, or some other locally available material. Bale walls are often also wrapped with 2-inch stucco mesh or chicken wire. Interior and exterior walls then receive coats of plaster or stucco, which give the walls a boost of shear strength. Various systems have been used to further bolster the shear values in seismically active areas. One common approach is to create a hybrid structure, where wood framed walls create structural strength and shear value as well as a rack for bales to be stacked in, while the in-fill straw walls provide the thick, sound-proof, highly

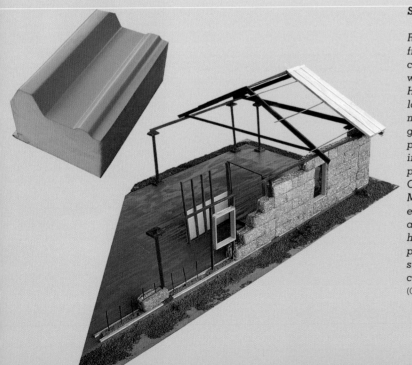

Steel-Framed Straw-Bale

Red iron is gaining favor as an alternative framing system for straw-bale construction to cut costs and speed the building process, as well as for its high recycled content. Heavy gauge steel is capable of supporting larger spans with relatively smaller members—eliminating the need for old-growth or glulams. While more advance planning is required, steel is more efficient in terms of jobsite waste, since materials are prefabricated to specifications. Complete Owner-Builder Systems of Santa Fe, New Mexico, now offers custom packages from engineering drawings through construction and financing for steel-framed straw-bale houses. A model of their patented system is pictured at left and includes a light-gauge steel roof system with foam R-50 panels called Galvanet, made in Monterrey, Mexico. (COBS, 505.466.1605 www.strawhouses.com)

Straw Dining Hall

Siegel & Strain Architects designed this red iron and straw-bale dining hall for a children's summer camp.

insulated properties people enjoy so much in these houses. Post-and-beam timber framing, as well as steel-framed solutions are also becoming increasingly common.

"Straw-bale building is still in a rapidly evolutionary state," explains David Eisenberg, co-author of the best-selling book, *The Straw Bale House*. Eisenberg believes that the next phase of straw-bale construction will involve creating systems that use the limitations of the bale itself to design and structural advantage. "Any modification of a bale—in terms of shortening it, adding moisture, rounding, or attaching it—takes time. And that often translates into more money. The best straw-bale systems recognize the modularity of the bale and try to work within it to minimize the cost of building. Unlike wood-framed housing systems, which have been refined over many decades, very few straw-bale projects have been very well optimized."

Others think we need to do more creative things with bales. "I think we could be building straw-bale infill skyscrapers," says David Arkin, by way of example. Architectural engineer, author and founding member of the California Straw Building Association Bruce King asserts that load-bearing straw-bale structures will be the wave of the future, once funding becomes available to complete the necessary testing and research. A hybrid of some sort—straw-bale and PISÉ (pneumatically impacted stabilized earth) or straw-bale and red iron framing, for example—may eventually bring natural building technologies to more and more homeowners and communities.

While the aesthetic, environmental, and personal values of straw-bale construction continue to attract increasing numbers of builders, and a large body of physical and anecdotal evidence is now available, many important questions remain. For example, in what regions of the country is straw-bale building appropriate? Will it be durable in wet climates, where moisture penetration might cause bales to decompose? How well will these structures hold up in regions of high seismic activity? Do post-and-beam and other hybrid framing structures really reduce the amount of wood compared with conventional stick-frame houses? What are the limits of load-bearing straw-bale structures? Will straw-bale homes always cost more than stick homes if contractor-built?

Whatever its direction, it is clear that straw-bale building will be with us for some time, as a new generation of homeowners, architects, and builders elects to go with what remains of the grain.

Municipal Sustainability

This watercolor rendering done by Santa Barbara-based architect Henry Lenny was proposed for a straw-bale public library that is yet to be built. The building is designed to create a power surplus.

Straw Appeal

Straw-bale lends itself to a variety of construction forms, rectilinear and otherwise. Deep window ledges are one of the benefits of its thick-walled construction. Generous roof overhangs are always recommended. Builders are continually pushing the limits of straw-bale's capabilities, with innovations from vaults to load-bearing palaces. (Photos: Bowman residence, Philo, California, 1; Real Goods Solar Living Center, Hopland, California, 2; Pape residence, Chama, New Mexico, 3; Branes and Arfa residence, Rancho de Cayucos, California, 4; San Luis Sustainability Group, 7).

Bale Built Winery

The Clairbourne and Churchill Winery in San Luis Obispo (photo 5) used straw-bale to create an all-purpose space for both a wine cellar and tasting room. An added bonus has been in the elimination of refrigeration for the wines. The temperature fluctuates between 60 and 65°F, adequate for maintaining quality fermentation.

Straw-Bale Remodel

Austin natural builder Frank Meyer used straw bales to build an addition to a conventional residence (photos 6 and 8), completely transforming a humble urban house into an exceptional space. Straw-bale walls have an estimated R-value of R-30 to R-50, and bring with them excellent acoustical properties as well.

Benefits: Block-making machines are portable, offering the ability to produce compressed earth blocks on-site and/or in remote areas. Very low embodied energy. Relatively fast earthen construction technique. Broad range of uses possible. With one inch of foam exterior insulation, can be thermally superior to wood construction in climates from Arizona to Minnesota. Can take advantage of unskilled labor.

Challenges: Unstabilized soil blocks can be vulnerable to moisture and must be protected from above and below. In the past, there has been difficulty in obtaining parts or maintenance for machines, although that seems to be improving. Often, soil must be excavated and brought on-site.

Applications: Latest technological developments improving dimensional accuracy of the blocks makes dry-stacking tongue and groove blocks possible. Applications for disaster relief and building in developing countries. Seismic studies currently underway to determine the applicability in earthquake-prone areas.

Bricks on Wheels

Machines that make hundreds of bricks per hour can be easily transported to the job site.

ON-SITE ADOBE

As one explores the world of clay building techniques, a wide range of variations on the straw clay theme unfolds. These include adobe (earth bricks, typically fortified with chopped straw), cob (an earth and straw mixture shaped into loaf-like elements), and wattle-and-daub (a woven wicker matrix onto which clay is applied). Most of these methods share the use of a clay sticky enough to bind with natural, locally available fibers. From there, techniques diverge. Bricks or blocks can be produced, then stacked and mortared. Wooden wall forms can be erected, filled, and compacted, a few feet at a time. Or walls can be sculpted in free-form fashion from handmade lumps. Adobe, the world's most adapted building method, is a venerable tradition that has a huge body of literature. In the following sections, we will focus on some of its lesser known earthen building relatives.

Like portable sawmills, new generations of mobile compressed soil block machines are making site-specific materials available to a broader range of builders and homeowners. Instead of turning trees into timbers and lumber, these mini-brick mills convert soil into a steady stream of blocks. Depending on the type of machine and builder, the blocks are sometimes 'stabilized' with between 5 and 10 percent cement; others are simply made of unstabilized earth. Advanced Earthen Construction Technologies (AECT) of San Antonio is the leading manufacturer of compressed soil block machines among 30 companies worldwide. AECT's machines, now sold in dozens of countries, can produce between 150 and 960 blocks per hour, depending on soil type and machine configuration. Compressed soil block machines are especially useful in remote areas where conventional adobes are unavailable.

"The ideal soil type has a powdery consistency, almost like flour, and is about 50 percent clay, 50 percent sand, with no more than 10 percent moisture," explains Joaquin Karcher, an architect and builder working in Taos, New Mexico. Karcher has designed and built 30 homes with compressed soil block machines over the past seven years. His buildings are typically dry-stacked (without mortar) and then stuccoed outside and plastered inside. In some cases, a breatheable urethane foam insulation was applied to the outside of the building to insulate against the temperature swings of the New Mexico climate. Karcher was drawn to this type of building by the very low embodied energy of the materials; the lack of toxic or energy-intensive stabilizers, such as the asphaltium and cement commonly added to adobe; and the ability to involve local labor. Even more, Karcher is inspired by the end result. "I'm concerned with the highest quality of building possible, and that includes healthy indoor air environments."

Tests have shown that compressed soil block buildings can be applicable to almost any climate, including rainforests and frozen areas. Newer machines are designed to be hauled around by a pickup. At 10 inches long, the blocks can be stacked to create thick walls, and are often built doubly thick for thermal mass or for aesthetics. Even dry-stacked walls with a concrete bond beam are fully load-bearing (depending on the region). They can also cost less than conventionally built frame and brick houses. Soil block houses are typically stuccoed on the outside and receive a plaster finish inside. Over 600 houses have been built in the United States. According to AECT, the houses are designed to last between 200 and 500 years.

Throughout the past few decades of start-ups, the compressed soil block industry has suffered a plethora of quality control problems, however, such as inconsistency of bricks, lack of parts and service for machines, and a dearth of construction standards. The industry appears to be maturing, however. AECT produces both massive, fast, production machines in the $200,000 range, and more portable, slower machines for $15,000 to $20,000. Foxfire Associates, of Middleburg, Virginia, is introducing a mortarless tongue-and-groove block system. That unit, dubbed the Green Machine, is manufactured by AECT and has already been experimented with by Habitat for Humanity, among others.

Karcher cautions that building with unstabilized bricks is not a worry-free process. "Because the bricks are vulnerable to rain, you have to erect the walls with a certain sense of urgency. The top layer of the wall should be covered and the concrete bond beam poured immediately. Then comes the roof, after which you can rest a little easier." In addition, Karcher offers the standard prescription for earthen buildings: appropriate source soils; a stem wall and moisture barrier that provides water protection from below; and a sound roof with generous overhangs to block all but driving rains.

While catching on in the southwestern United States, proponents believe that the primary market for this technology will be in developing countries. The mobility and quality of the emerging technology suggests that the technique could be extremely successful in the rest of the United States if machines were made available by large building supply chains on a rental basis. This could make following in the footsteps of Egyptian, Etruscan, and Roman builders as easy as renting the machine, hiring an excavator or front loading tractor, and rolling up your sleeves.

Earth Blocks

These are particularly suited to earthen building forms prevalent in the architecture of the southwestern and western United States.
Laid on edge, they create a dynamic floor pattern in Joaquin Karcher's Taos passive solar residence.
Bricks can be dry-stacked in certain regions, and double-stacked for superior thermal performance.

Adobe Interior

These two photos on the top right show traditional adobe interior walls in the Pape residence, which combined a number of natural building methods, including straw- bale.

Bond Beam Prep

Workers complete the forms to pour the concrete bond beam atop this dry-stacked soil block wall.

Benefits: Little construction waste. Extremely durable. Opportunities for sweat equity. Good thermal performance in temperate areas. Excess material can be used for landscaping elements. Fly ash can be substituted for cement content. Forms are typically reused.

Challenges: Embodied energy can be higher than conventional building in seismically active regions, although this is often offset by durability. Sometimes involves mining of off-site soil and/or minerals, such as decomposed granite, for texture, color, and consistency. Costs are somewhat higher than many other approaches.

Applications: In western Australia, where rammed earth construction has gained a skilled labor force and capitalization, it has become cost-competitive for residential as well as commercial structures. Can be specified under building codes in most areas including regions of heavy seismic activity.

Ramming and Jamming

Formwork systems for rammed earth are rapidly evolving in western Australia as well as the United States. This PISÉ wall is being erected using the Rammed Earth Works continuous form system, utilizing high-density overlay plywood, rebar, and pipe clamps.
The nozzleman blasts on the material while finishers quickly trowel it to a smooth surface. Excess material is often used to form pavers and other landscaping materials.

MANMADE SEDIMENTARY ROCK

Perhaps no one else in the United States has brought more attention to the tradition of earthen structures than Napa builder and industrial engineer David Easton. For decades he and others have been battling the stigma that earth is only for the dirt poor and, in fact, his rammed earth and PISÉ (pneumatically impacted stabilized earth) homes are among the most beautiful buildings of any style being constructed today.

While rammed earth's traditions spring from such massive structures as the pyramids and sections of the Great Wall of China (which have survived without the fortification of rebar, cement, and other recent innovations), its modern revival originated in the 1970s with simultaneous movements on three continents: Australia, Europe, and North America. Today there are two primary approaches to rammed earth construction in North America. One involves pouring the material into a monolithic wall form and ramming it using a pneumatic compactor. This is employed by a number of contractors in various parts of the country. PISÉ, Easton's personal approach, is blasted onto a rebar framework through a pneumatic nozzle, then troweled to a smooth exterior finish. Easton derived inspiration for his acronym from the French term for rammed earth construction, *pisé de terre*.

The use of modern tractors, mixing equipment, and pneumatic ramming tools has increased the speed of the otherwise very labor-intensive production process of rammed earth and PISÉ. The incorporation of mined materials such as decomposed granite has also helped to achieve sophisticated textures, consistent mixtures, and specific color schemes.

According to Easton, there are particular reasons that rammed earth construction has really taken off in Australia, while remaining just a fringe building technique in isolated areas of the United States, and languishing in France, where some of the greatest early examples remain. In western Australia, a ravenous termite population precludes the use of wood walls in any form; there, rammed earth provides so many benefits to homeowners that once launched as a viable alternative to brick wall construction, it quickly captured as much as 20 percent of the market in some areas.[1]

At its most basic, rammed earth is soil packed between temporary forms to create thick walls. When up to 20 percent cement is added to sandy clay or clayey sand, and the material is either pneumatically tamped or blasted with a nozzle onto a rebar-reinforced form, it essentially becomes a form of stratified rock. Depending on the colors of the earthen materials used, the strata appear in the walls in fluid tones like a sand painting or canyon wall.

Not all building sites have soils ideal for rammed earth, and choosing the proper wall material is best done from a scientific perspective. Easton leans toward quarry 'fines,' a byproduct of decorative rock mining, in addition to sandy clays or clayey sands, with a well-graded blend of different-size soil particles. Sand and gravel provide the aggregate, while the clay and water act as glue. Cement increases strength, durability, and moisture resistance. Agricultural soils—slowly renewed and as valuable as petroleum—are not good for earth buildings because they are usually high in tilth but lacking appropriate structure. Easton's book, *The Rammed Earth House*, offers a detailed analysis on the subject of soils as well as discussing every other aspect of rammed earth construction.

"The one thing you have to understand as a homeowner is that you can't expect perfection from rammed earth quite like the precise tolerances available from many manufactured materials," explains Easton. "But some beautiful unexpected qualities appear as the material settles over time. A building develops a character all its own through the natural processes of weathering, and occasional chipping and spalling."

Easton is among a handful of specialists in various areas of the United States who collectively complete some three dozen rammed earth homes per year. An industrial engineer with a background in technology development, he became interested in rammed earth as a cost-effective owner-builder technique. Once he gained experience working with the material first-hand, Easton began pursuing the advancement of the formwork technology in the hopes of creating an affordable rammed earth system, thinking he would soon move on to something else. Instead, rammed earth became both a career and a calling. Easton spent nearly ten years experimenting with systems to make rammed earth affordable and high quality. Since the early 1990s, he has been building his unique PISE-wall homes for clients throughout Northern California.

Unfortunately, affordability hasn't yet materialized for PISÉ, at least not in the United States. At $28 to $30 a square foot, it is easily among the most expensive wall systems—but with a 500-year life expectancy, also among the most durable.

A great deal of the artistry and labor costs of rammed earth lies in the form work. Even with a team of highly skilled journeymen, only about 300 square feet of wall surface per day can be erected. The walls for a home can take as long as three weeks to form, but then they are also finished surfaces, requiring no plaster, drywall, paint, siding, etc—inside or out.

Easton's PISÉ technology is based on swimming pool and tunnel casing construction. It involves the use of a gunite hose to blast the rammed earth mixture onto a form wall; the exposed wall surface is then troweled and screeded to a clean and angular finish. PISÉ, Easton argues, increases the speed, ease, and consistency of a project. Witnessing a PISÉ wall being built is a spectacle of intensity. Loaders hustle to keep materials moving into the mixer, which feeds the rammed earth into the hose, while the nozzleman, hose coiled and braced around one leg, blasts wads of mixed sand, clay, decomposed granite, and cement onto the wall form. A clean-up team quickly follows, shoveling and troweling and trimming the lumpy earthen layers into smooth, angular wall surfaces that look hundreds of years old on the day they are erected.

How does PISÉ rank in terms of materials and embodied energy? Where earthquake requirements are high, Easton explains, the embodied energy (due to the cement content) can be greater than a conventional stick-framed wall. However, when viewed in terms of its 500-year, low-maintenance life expectancy, it measures up well. For Easton, longevity is more than enough reason to justify its use.

Easton is doubtful of the probability of any major shift away from the dominance of wood-based construction occurring in the near future, given the huge numbers of carpenters and the establishment of the industry. "They'll switch to all plastic studs before making any significant changes," he predicts, "but we'll continue doing what we do, demonstrating that alternatives do indeed have a place in contemporary construction."

California or France?

David Easton's PISÉ (pneumatically impacted stabilized earth) work can be seen throughout Northern California in a wide range of spectacular building projects. Easton's Napa home, (all pictures but the two on the far upper right which are of the Scharffenberger house in Philo) showcases the versatility of rammed earth, from walls to floors to window and door frames to landscaping.

Enduring Elegance

Rammed earth structures are estimated to last five hundred years. Engineering data is now accumulating on modern rammed earth structures representing a broad range of geographic and performance variables. As demonstrated here, the material can be not only be extremely durable, but elegant.

Benefits: Excellent examples of light straw clay walls have survived centuries in Europe. Thick walls provide insulation and mass. Costs can be competitive with high-end custom homes. Can reduce the amount of wood in a structure depending on the load-bearing system.

Challenges: Extremely labor-intensive. Walls can take months to dry out and cure in certain areas. Obtaining proper quality clay materials can take time, excavation, and/or transportation. Standard stick-frame construction may require more wood to frame for attaching wall forms.

Applications: Some extremely beautiful custom residences and additions are being constructed today in many areas of the country. Infill for post-and-beam structures. Lends itself to rectilinear designs. State of New Mexico's Construction Industries Division has published standards for non-load-bearing light straw clay construction, entitled *Clay Straw Guidelines*.

Technologically Appropriate

This tumbler to blend straw and clay slip was devised by New Mexico architect, Alfred von Bachmayr. It's portable and mechanizes the task of mixing materials. Not to worry, there's still plenty of manual labor involved in the light straw clay system.

CLAY ON A HIGH FIBER DIET

While straw-bale has certainly basked in the natural building movement's limelight over the past several years, one wall system garnering increasing interest is light straw clay, known also as light clay or straw clay. The name 'light clay,' according to practitioners Robert Laporte and Frank Andresen, derives from the German *leichtlehm*, which translates as 'light loam,' and is a practice with roots going back in some form or another for as long as humans have been building. In essence, light straw clay is a marriage of basic materials: straw for its insulating and tensile properties, with earth for its characteristic mass. The light straw clay process involves coating five parts straw fibers (or wood chips) with one part liquified clay ('slip'), then packing, tamping, and sometimes ramming the mixture between wall forms or into blocks or panels.

Robert Laporte became a convert to light clay building on a trip to Germany some years ago. On that journey, he visited an 800-year-old house, where one of the traditional earthen walls had been opened up for repairs. "Inside those wattle-and-daub straw and clay walls was a willow whip that was still green after eight centuries. That convinced me more than anything that the longevity of a structure is directly proportionate to how well it breathes," says Laporte. Over the past six years, he and his Tesuque, New Mexico-based company have been building 'Econests'—small but comfortable timber frame homes with walls of light straw clay. Econests are usually completed through workshops.

"These walls have several characteristics," explains Laporte. "They are permeable. They provide mass. The straw insulates, strengthens, and absorbs sound, while the clay acts as a glue. And finally, they are hygroscopic, meaning they will resist fire and mold, and moderate humidity within the building." Laporte, who helped draft New Mexico's state building code for non-load-bearing light clay, explains that studs are required every 32 inches, primarily as a fastener for formwork. In addition, 'blind studs' are used to frame doors and windows, and bamboo canes are placed horizontally within the wall sections as they are raised to provide vertical stability.

While the light straw clay mixture was once mixed laboriously with a pitchfork, a new, low-tech tumbler, invented by architect Alfred von Bachmayr, now speeds the process along. Forms are used to raise the thick walls two feet at a time, and as soon as one level is formed, drained, and tamped by feet and tools, the next level is added. "Always keep the entire wall form up until the wall reaches its full height," cautions Laporte. The walls of a 1,400-square-foot light straw clay home usually take two weeks to infill. A few weeks later the entire wall can sprout to a living green, and then take several more months to completely dry out, even in a desert climate.

"If I've learned anything during my years as a builder, it's that something healthy is something that's alive," says Laporte. "And if you want to build a healthy house, then you should build it as much as possible with living materials."

Natural Systems

The Econest Building Company favors timber framing and light straw clay infill walls. This detail of a timber frame in progress shows Robert Laporte's expert joinery. The walls will be raised with light straw clay infill using stackable forms (see photo, right). Light straw clay walls can take up to eight months to dry properly. The photo of the finished house above shows an unplastered, light straw clay Econest that has weathered well for a number of years in southern New Mexico.

THE TIMBER FRAME ECONEST

"Particularly at a time when resource conservation is so essential, we have the responsibility to use wood wisely and to do something well," says Robert Laporte, a timber framer and founder of the Econest Building Company in Tesuque, New Mexico. "I have made my peace with working with wood by building structures designed to last five centuries. Most of the trees in my timber frames are between 60 and 80 years old," explains Laporte, "while the structure should last many more times that."

A forester by training, Laporte tired of the excessive office work required by the job and started timber framing two decades ago. He says he's learned most of what he knows by "listening to the wood." He credits the Timber Framers Guild for furthering his knowledge, and Masahiko (a Japanese master carpenter) for his inspiration. Laporte obtains most of his timbers from forester Harry Morrisson, in Chama, New Mexico, whose forestry practices he knows extremely well. "You can hike enjoyably in his forestlands," says Laporte.

The desire to make high quality, ecologically responsible homes affordable to a broader range of people led Laporte to found the Econest Building Company. His wife, architect and author Paula Baker Laporte, designs the houses. 'Econests' are generally 1,400 square feet or less and are made with a minimal amount of manufactured products, and feature timber frame structures (in the Japanese tradition) and breathable, light straw clay walls.

"Today the longevity of a building is conventionally measured by how well the building is sealed," says Laporte, "which is basically the same as putting it in a garbage bag and stamping a date on it. The longevity of a building is actually proportionate to how well it breathes," says Laporte, and for that reason he usually uses light straw clay walls for the New Mexico climate where he does much of his building.

Laporte says that making a life of timber framing and natural building has made him a better person. "Timber framing has changed my standards. It builds me as a human being and makes me feel more connected to the planet. There is a learning process of working with these natural materials that somehow gives me a greater sense of belonging. What incentive is there in being the best stick framer on the planet? Your work is finished as fast as possible and then is just covered up with manufactured materials."

According to Laporte, the foundation, framing, and light straw clay wall system comprise between 25 and 30 percent of the cost of a building. "But that 30 percent captures the soul of the house. People ask me how they can afford such luxurious structures. But, considering all we know, I wonder how we can afford not to invest in the soul of a home."

Built-in Comfort

Econests are designed to be small but homey. The use of classic geometry and many functional built-ins and copious natural lighting gives a generous feel to a compact space.

East Meets West

Econest building geometry and certain room styles are decidedly Asian in influence, including rooms with tatami mat floors and shoji screens. Others, like the kitchen (below), are contemporary Western.

Nesting Headquarters

The Tesuque, New Mexico, headquarters of the Econest Building Company and Baker Laporte Associates combines the timeless features of timber framing and light clay infill walls.

Earth Floors and Plasters

Earthen plasters are used inside and out in a variety of colors and textures. Artisans throughout the Southwest are reviving the craft of traditional mud flooring and earth plastering.

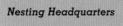

Benefits: Highly sculptural, forgiving, and controllable material. A wide range of soil types can be used, making site or local materials an option. Easy to learn, teach, and repair. Excellent thermal mass. Amenable to ornamentation, pigmentation, and mosaics. Durable and fire-resistant.

Challenges: Slow and labor-intensive. As a contemporary building system, it is relatively experimental and further research is needed with respect to seismic performance, moisture resistance, and other critical factors. Mechanization and other innovations are needed to make cob more widely applicable. Raw materials are heavy; can be difficult to transport.

Applications: While often used for whole buildings, cob's best application may be as an interior component of other hybrid systems. Ideal for south-facing thermal mass walls, built-in hearths, benches, hutches, and other applications.

Just Add Water

The construction site for cob buildings can be relatively simple. In many cases, the straw and clay are mixed by feet and hand tools. This residence designed, by Austin architect Gayle Borst, was being built by cob contractor Mike Carter, who speeds up the production process with electric cement mixers.

THE HANDMADE POTTERY OF BUILDING

No other form of earthen construction seems to deviate from rectilinear forms so much as the fluid, free-form method of cob. Like its close relatives, adobe and rammed earth, cob ranks among the oldest traditional building approaches, combining clay and sand with water and straw. The name comes from the Old English, meaning 'lump or rounded mass'—and that, in essence, describes the method of hand sculpting structures with individual loaves of fibrous mud. Also like rammed earth and adobe, cob is a load-bearing wall system that can drastically reduce the need for wood in a building.

Unlike adobe, which is formed into blocks and dried, cob is applied while moist. The malleable nature of the fresh material lends itself to sculptural detailing and spontaneous creativity. It is perhaps this quality that most often draws people to cob. While sometimes used for entire structures, it is often used to create individual elements in a natural building project, such as built-in benches, fireplaces, or garden walls. For mud lovers, cob may be the ultimate party medium, engaging participants in stomping and molding the stiff loaves and tossing them in bucket-brigade fashion to the wall building site. Because of its putty-like plasticity and ability to adhere to straw, wood, and most other natural materials, cob is sometimes referred to as 'the duct tape of natural building.'

According to Michael G. Smith, author and natural builder, the exact origins of cob are unknown. Perhaps its value as a mortar for stone construction caused some to experiment with it as a load-bearing wall system.

Whatever its origins, cob emerged as a popular English building system by 1500 A.D., producing thick-walled structures—often up to three feet—with no bricks, mortar, or wooden framing, until it was displaced by the Industrial Revolution's mass-produced bricks.

Today cob is experiencing a slow, quiet revival in both England and North America. Interest in the technique is rising in traditional English cob centers, such as Devon, which is home to an estimated 20,000 structures, some of which are now being restored. Thanks to this restoration work, a fair amount of research and documentation is currently underway in Britain. In Oregon, Ianto Evans, Linda Smiley, and Smith sparked an owner-builder cob movement with specific techniques for building in seismic areas, which has branched out through workshops in various regions of the United States and abroad.

Even when compared to its natural building method relatives, cob is extremely slow and labor-intensive. Traditionally, cob was shoveled into place, then stamped onto the walls by workers. Today, attempts are being made to speed up the process with portable mixers and other mechanizing innovations.

Mike Carter, a computer engineer turned cob contractor, has completed a number of interesting projects in and around Austin. According to Carter, who uses an electric mixer ("quiet and wildlife friendly but not as efficient as an expensive mortar mixer"), the load-bearing cob walls are one of the easier parts of his building process. "The foundation and roof system give me many more headaches than the walls, which are really just the building's insulation," says Carter.

Like any good builder, Carter emphasizes the foundation and roof details, for good reason. One of the primary enemies of cob construction is prolonged soaking. Preventing moisture from entering the wall near the base of the structure, where loads are greatest, as well as from running down the wall or entering from above, is critical.

Anyone interested in cob construction can benefit from Michael G. Smith's outstanding and inspiring workshops and books, *The Cobber's Companion* and *The Cob Cottage: A Philosophical and Practical Guide to Building an Ecstatic House*, which explain in great detail and with great pleasure the ins and outs of building a lasting, aesthetically pleasing—and completely recyclable—house of cob.

Cob Compound

Cottages at Emerald Earth in Boonville, California, use cob, 'clay wattle,' and straw bale. Note the living roof and site-milled timbers.

The Essence is in the Details

The easy-to-apply nature of cob lends itself to the handmade; not just free flowing walls, but built-in and sculptural nooks, hutches, book cases, windows, and hearths, to name just a few. At The Occidental Arts and Ecology Center, Occidental, California, a cob cottage known as 'the Hermitage' was constructed through numerous workshops.(Top three photos.)

Cob Office

Gardner Imhoff checking out the cob office and studio of the Permaculture Institute, Pt. Reyes, California, (photo above, far right).

Nooks and Books

In recent years, the revival of traditional earthen plasters and clay slip (aliz) by such artisans as Carole Crews is changing the finishes of natural building. (Photo, bottom left) By searching out specifically colored clays or adding pigments, a variety of tones can be achieved to create smooth, dust-free, glimmering surfaces. (Ekedal residence, Tres Orejas, New Mexico)

Handcrafted Hearth

Frank Meyer chose cob to make this elegant hearth on a remodel in Austin, Texas. This demonstrates the sophisticated design potentials of the material.

The family of natural building organizations is wide-ranging. There are essentially groups in every region of the country and an increasing number of workshops and gatherings where hands-on experience and technical discussions can critically flesh out advantages and disadvantages of different building approaches. These groups are continually keeping up with structural issues and construction techniques and serve as valuable information centers.

The following list of organizations comes courtesy of author Michael G. Smith. The selected listing of natural building resources are reprinted with permission from Black Range Lodge Natural Building Resources Center in Kingston, New Mexico and The Last Straw Journal. Many more resources are available through the publishers, distributors, and websites listed in this section.

BLACK RANGE LODGE NATURAL BUILDING RESOURCES
Kingston, New Mexico
505.895.5652
www.strawbalecentral.com
Straw-bale resources, videos, and natural building colloquiums.

CALIFORNIA EARTH ART AND ARCHITECTURE INSTITUTE
Hesperia, California
760.244.0614
www.calearth.org
Center for earthbag construction founded by Nader Khalili.

CALIFORNIA STRAW BUILDING ASSOCIATION
Angels Camp, California
209.785.7077
www.strawbuilding.org
Regional straw-bale association with a research focus.

THE CANELO PROJECT
Elgin, Arizona
520.455.5548
www.caneloproject.com
Innovative low-cost housing using local and natural resources.

CENTER FOR MAXIMUM POTENTIAL BUILDING SYSTEMS
Austin, Texas
512.928.4786
www.cmpbs.org
Leading research on materials and building design.

COB COTTAGE COMPANY
Cottage Grove, Oregon
541.942.2005
www.deatech.com/cobcottage
Workshops and resources for cob construction.

COMMUNITY ECODESIGN NETWORK
Minneapolis, Minnesota
612.722.3260
www.cedn.org
Regional straw-bale workshops. Testing and experimentation for the upper midwestern climate.

CRATerre
Maison Levrat, France
33.474.954391
www.grenoble.archi.fr
Focus on earthen architecture for international development.

DEVELOPMENT CENTER FOR APPROPRIATE TECHNOLOGY
Tucson, Arizona
520.624.6628
www.azstarnet.com/~dcat
www.dcat.net
Focus on natural building and greening of building codes.

ECONEST BUILDING COMPANY
Tesuque, New Mexico
505.984.2928
505.989.1813
Pbaker@trail.com
Workshops on timber framing and light straw clay construction.

ECOLOGICAL BUILDING NETWORK
Sausalito, California
415.331.7630
www.ecobuildingnetwork.org
Research organization for structural testing and new materials.

ECOLOGICAL DESIGN INSTITUTE
Sausalito, California
415.332.5806
www.ecodesign.org
Natural building institute and press founded by Sim Van der Ryn.

THE FARM
ECOVILLAGE TRAINING CENTER
Summertown, Tennessee
931.964.4474
www.thefarm.org/etc
Workshops and resources for ecological communities.

FOX MAPLE SCHOOL OF
TRADITIONAL BUILDING
West Brownfield, Maine
207.935.3720
www.foxmaple.com
Workshops on timber framing and
traditional infill systems.

GROUNDWORKS
Murphys, Oregon
541.471.3470
www.cpros.com/~sequoia
Cob workshops and information.

HEARTWOOD SCHOOL
Washington, Massachusetts
413.623.6677
www.heartwoodschool.com
Courses in alternative building
methods including timber framing
and straw-bale.

INTERNATIONAL INSTITUTE FOR
BAU-BIOLOGIE & ECOLOGY
Clearwater, Florida
www.bau-biologieusa.com
Resources and education on the
principles of healthy building.

OCCIDENTAL ARTS AND
ECOLOGY CENTER
Occidental, California
707.874.1557
www.oaec.org
Organization dedicated to
education, ecological communities, permaculture, natural
building, and art.

OUT ON BALE, UNLIMITED
Tucson, Arizona
520.624.1673 / 520.622.6896
ww.greenbuilder.com/dawn
Straw-bale education, consulting,
publishing, wall raisings.

RAMMED EARTH WORKS
Napa, California
707.224.2532
rew@interx.net
Leading company in development of earth construction technology.

REAL GOODS INSTITUTE FOR
SOLAR LIVING
Hopland, California
707.744.2017
www.solarliving.org
Workshops on natural building and
annual summer solstice festival.

ROCKY MOUNTAIN INSTITUTE
Green Development Services
Snowmass, Colorado
970.927.3851
www.rmi.org
Resources on sustainable
building and renewable energy.

SOLAR ENERGY
INTERNATIONAL
Carbondale, Colorado
970.963.8855
www.solarenergy.org
Trainings and resources on alternative energy and construction.

SOUTHWEST SOLAR ADOBE
SCHOOL
Bosque, New Mexico
505.861.1255
www.adobebuilder.com
Resources and workshops on
adobe and earthen construction.

YESTERMORROW DESIGN/BUILD
SCHOOL
Warren, Vermont
802.496.5540 / 888.496.5541
www.yestermorrow.org
Courses in all aspects of ecological design and construction.

Natural Building Books/Manuals/Videos

ALTERNATIVE CONSTRUCTION:
Contemporary Natural Building
Methods
Edited by Lynne Elizabeth and
Cassandra Adams
John Wiley and Sons
212.850.6000
www.wiley.com

THE ART OF NATURAL
BUILDING: Design, Construction,
Technology
Edited by Joseph F. Kennedy
New Society Publishers
www.newsociety.com

CERAMIC HOUSES: How to Build
Your Own
Nader Khalili
Harper & Row

THE COBBER'S COMPANION:
How to Build Your Own Earthen
Home
Michael G. Smith
Cob Cottage Company
541.942.2005
www.deatech.com/cobcottage

THE EARTH BUILDERS'
ENCYCLOPEDIA
Joseph Tibbets
Southwest Solar Adobe School
505.861.1255
www.adobebuilder.com

EARTH PLASTERS FOR STRAW
BALE HOMES
Keely Meagan
www.dirtcheapbuilder.com

EARTHEN FLOORS
Athena and Bill Steen
The Canelo Project
520.455.5548
www.caneloproject.com

THE LAST STRAW
The Grassroots Journal of Straw-
Bale and Natural Building
505.895.5400
www.strawhomes.com

STRAW BALE CONSTRUCTION
AND THE BUILDING CODES
David Eisenberg
Development Center for
Appropriate Technology
520.624.6628
www.dcat.net
www.azstarnet.com/~dcat

STRAW BALE CONSTRUCTION:
Beautiful Sustainable Buildings
Straw House Herbals
902.845.2750
www.shipharbour@ns.sympatico.ca

STRAW BALE HOUSE PLANS
Pueblo Habitat for Humanity
719.546.1341
www.moxvox.com
geiger-shinn@amigo.net

A VISUAL PRIMER TO STRAW-
BALE CONSTRUCTION
Steve MacDonald
Builders without Borders
www.builderswithoutborders.org

Following materials available through Black Range Lodge
505.895.5652
www.strawbalecentral.com

BUILDINGS OF EARTH AND STRAW: Structural Design for Rammed Earth and Straw-Bale Architecture
Bruce King, P.E.

HOW TO BUILD STRAW BALE Landscape and Privacy Walls
Tim Farrant

STRAW BALE BUILDING: How to Plan, Design and Build with Straw
Chris Magwood and Peter Mack

STRAW BALE CONSTRUCTION: A Manual for Maritime Regions
Kim Thompson, et al

STRAW BALE BUILDING AND THE CODES: Working With Your Code Officials
David Eisenberg

STRAW BALE CONSTRUCTION DETAILS: A Sourcebook
Edited by Ken Haggard and Scott Clarck

A STRAW BALE HOME TOUR
(video)
Tours of 10 homes with comments from owners and builders.

THE STRAW BALE SOLUTION
(video)
Narrated by Athena and Bill Steen.

A STRAW BALE WORKSHOP
(video)
Basics of straw-bale construction through step-by-step building of a two-story post-and-beam greenhouse.

Following materials available through Chelsea Green Publishing
802.295.6300
www.chelseagreen.com

BUILD IT WITH BALES: A Step-by-Step Guide to Straw Bale Construction, Version Two
S.O. MacDonald and Matts Myhrman

THE COB COTTAGE: A Philosophical and Practical Guide to Building an Ecstatic House
Michael G. Smith

THE NATURAL HOUSE: A Complete Guide to Healthy, Energy-Efficient, Environmental Homes
Daniel D. Chiras

THE RAMMED EARTH HOUSE
David Easton

THE STRAW BALE HOUSE
Athena and Bill Steen, David Bainbridge and David Eisenberg

Following materials available through Sustainable Systems Support
520.432.4292
www.bisbeenet.com/buildnatural
sssalive@primenet.com

HOW TO BUILD YOUR ELEGANT HOME WITH STRAW BALES
Steve Kemble and Carol Escott Video and manual set for load-bearing construction.

STRAW-BALE HOME PLANS
Stephen A. Kemble, Jr. P.E.

STRAW BALE CONSTRUCTION: The Elegant Solution
(video)
History and discussion.

Websites

www.balewatch.com
Robert Andrew's Straw Bale
719.561.8020 / 719.546.0315
Over 60 house plans, many links to other natural building sites.

www.dirtcheapbuilder.com
Home of Taylor Publishing, source for many hard-to-find natural building books, pictures, and other useful information.

www.eren.doe.gov
Energy Efficiency and Renewable Energy Clearinghouse (EREC)
800.363.3732
A comprehensive resource from the U.S. Department of Energy. Search for 'natural building.'

www. sustainableABC.com
Sustainable building and culture website. Information and links for straw-bale construction.

RECYCLED MATERIALS AND RESOURCE

RECOVERY

An economic system strung out on global clearcutting and seemingly limitless landfill space is predicated on many unfortunate and unacknowledged costs. One of these is to make it very difficult to develop local sources of recycled-content products at prices competitive with virgin materials—particularly wood. Not only are trees undervalued for the full spectrum of ecological services they provide, but their fiber all too frequently ends up being wasted, buried, or burned. Construction waste and demolition debris—up to 40 percent of it wood—account for a little over one-third of the continual flow into North America's burgeoning and bloated garbage pits. An estimated 300 million shipping pallets are produced every year, said to contain up to 1.5 billion feet of usable (mostly hardwood) lumber;[1] less than 20 percent of this material is recycled, and half is burned for fuel. Land clearing for development creates mountains of unused wood. Per capita, U.S. citizens annually dispose of approximately 300 pounds of waste paper, as well as another 40 pounds of plastics and one worn-out tire.[2] Slowly and steadily, landfills are becoming virtual Fort Knoxes of recoverable and reusable materials, rich in metals and chockful of wood, plastics, rubber, and other non-garbage. Diverting materials from landfills has the potential to decrease the demand for virgin materials—as well as energy—since, in general, recycling is less energy-intensive than processing and manufacturing virgin resources.

CONSTRUCTION AND DEMOLITION WASTE

The good news is that resource recovery models are emerging that could be replicated in metropolitan areas throughout the country. In some California cities and counties, for example, reclamation of wood resources is required whenever demolition or remodeling permits are issued. The Whole House Building Supply in East Palo Alto takes this one step further, conducting well-publicized and highly successful salvage auctions nearly every week. Entire roof assemblies, vintage wooden floors, doors, windows, cabinetry, bathrooms, lighting fixtures, stained glass, landscaping materials, and other elements can be obtained. Subscribers to the Northern California Architects/ Designers/Planners for Social Responsibility listserv (www.adpsr-norcal.org) receive detailed announcements along the following lines:

> "The house is a 5,000 sq. ft Monterey Mission Style house built in 1929 and added onto in 1945. The features (are you ready for this?): mission (barrel shaped) roof tiles, beautiful vertical grain fir cabinets, hand painted Mexican tiles, multi-paned wood doors & windows, milky glass knobs, handles & light fixtures, crystal & clear glass knobs, old tub & pedestal sink, ..."

According to the Natural Resources Defense Council, "Wood waste, the largest contributor to job-site refuse, can be reduced drastically and save builders hundreds of dollars on avoided landfill costs on a single job." Their handbook, *Efficient Wood Use in Residential Construction* (1998), offers contractors a detailed list of strate-gies to set up a construction and demolition recycling program on the job site that can save resources, energy, and money.

RECYCLED WOOD PRODUCTS

While perhaps not as environmentally preferable as FSC-certified or salvaged materials, recycled-wood-containing building products are definitely worthy of research and support. Industrial scraps, municipal solid waste, urban tree waste, and demolition debris can be transformed into usable materials. Sawdust, for example, can be incorporated into window frames and sills, door cores, and particleboard construction; cut-offs of 2x4s and 2x6s can be pieced together into finger-jointed studs, flooring, and trim materials; wood chips can be blended into plastic lumber, cementitious siding, roof tiles, and industrial panelboards. Search out products, resources, and suppliers that use recycled wood materials and specify them when appropriate. (See pages 116-131).

RECYCLED-CONTENT MANUFACTURED MATERIALS

The range and number of manufactured recycled-content materials entering the construction market is growing all the time. These include products made from recovered plastics, wood, newsprint, fly ash, blast furnace slag, styrofoam, paper pulp sludge, wood lignin, concrete, rubber, tire shreds, carpeting, glass, and agricultural residues, to name just a few.

John Barrie Associates Architects, an Ann Arbor, Michigan, firm with a green building focus, regularly specifies recycled materials, many of which substitute for wood. Some of their standard specifications include:

- recycled-content wood-plastic composite decking;
- recycled nylon carpets;
- cellulose insulation;
- fly ash and blast furnace slag to replace some cement content in concrete;
- light-gauge steel, red iron, and metal roofing, all of which usually have significant recycled content;
- doors with post-industrial scrap in core materials (such as Thermatrue or Weyerhauser);
- Thermo-ply sheathing as a substitute for plywood sheathing and siding;
- recycled-content radiant barriers and acoustical barriers;
- fiber-cement composite siding materials;
- sheetrock with a high percentage of recycled core material and 100 percent recycled paper facings;
- asphalt shingles with 100 percent recycled paper core;
- countertops made from 'ag residues' and other recycled-content materials;
- recycled paint (of which there are between 50 and 100 manufacturers).

RECYCLING'S CATCH-22

Given the scope and scale of ecological threats such as biodiversity loss, global warming, and cumulative toxic pollution of all kinds, it is easy, perhaps, to make too much of recycling. The root causes of these problems won't be addressed no matter how many tons of milk bottles we convert into decking materials and synthetic fleece, or how much straw we use for wall boards and paper pulp. The fact remains, however, that taking optimal advantage of those resources we do exploit could discourage logging, generate revenue to support recycling systems, and help protect ecosystems.

MINING THE URBAN WASTE STREAM

Outside the CAN Fibre particleboard facility in Riverside, California, is a mountain of wood scraps being added to and diminished by a small army of Bobcats feeding numerous conveyor systems. Each day, hundreds of tons of wood scrap from the surrounding metropolitan areas are sorted, chopped, cleaned, washed, and finally pulverized into fine consistent fibers, then mixed with a phenol formaldehyde binder and hot-pressed into medium-density fiber board. At the end of the production line, 3/4-inch sheets, 8 feet wide and 24 feet long peel off like giant graham crackers, destined to become cabinetry, furniture, moldings, door jams, and shelves. A second plant is planned for Lackawanna, New York.

MARLY PORTER'S 'PORTA-HOUSE'

While opening up an office on the site of the now well-known One World Theater in Austin, Texas, architect Marly Porter became convinced of the merits of building small and designing around the principle of impermanence. Porter, who was commuting at the time, spent ten days per month living and operating out of a trailer, and found it provided everything he needed. "Who's to say that we should be building structures to last indefinitely?" asks Porter. "What about creating homes or modular rooms that can be hoisted onto a trailer and hauled to a different location?"

In addition to reclaiming materials as much as possible, Porter is an ardent believer that some entire buildings should be 'recyclable,' too. His current home is a small cluster of unconnected rooms that have been constructed to be taken away should his need for them cease. There's an eight-by-eight-foot bathroom built primarily of reclaimed and recycled materials, with the tops of the walls splayed out to give the illusion of a grander space. It also has a deck on top with a view of downtown Austin. The bedroom is 12 by 16 feet, including the closet, all designed around the Chinese organizing principles of *feng shui*. His son lives in a ten-by-ten treehouse reached by a discarded spiral staircase. A 12 by 24 foot kitchen and dining room, complete with loft, services the compound.

"I suspect that these rooms will all be moved one day," says Porter. "One of my kids will get the bathroom, another the bedroom, and the other the guest room."

Marly Porter's work can be seen at *www.livingarchitecture.com*.

When remodeling the kitchen in their Berkeley, California, home, Randy Hester and Marcia McNally envisioned an environmentally oriented solution, right down to the exterior wall finish. They called on architects Anni Tilt and David Arkin to spearhead the project. Their first inspiration came from a relic homestead in California's former gold country.

"There is a building in the ghost town of Bodie sheathed in tin cans," explained Arkin. "But a sample panel rusted within three weeks in our salty, smoggy, Bay Area environment."

They settled on license plates instead. Six hundred to be exact, many found through a friend of Hester in North Carolina who owns a car dealership. The siding job took three days of careful labor. They also scavenged a piece of railroad track with an 1882 birthmark for an I-roof beam, used off-cuts of salvaged lumber for siding and trim, and turned to a local artisan for a countertop containing recycled glass (see page 127).

This relatively small job points to the great imagination that can be applied in bringing principles of non-wood, recycled, environmentally preferable materials to the task of building.

Contact www.arkintilt.com.

EXTREME SALVAGE

It takes big vision to think small, think local, and demand waste as a primary resource material. It was the tremendous mountains of rubble resulting from the devastating 1991 Northridge earthquake, combined with a profound admiration for Iberian stone architecture, that inspired the vision that Yvon and Melinda Chouinard created for a house perched on a wild property on the California coastline. They told architect Robert Mehl and contractor Kit Boise-Cossart they wanted a small house that would fit intimately into the bluff above the ocean; recycled materials were to be used whenever possible, and absolutely no virgin timbers were to be felled for the project. "We built a house from a lot of junk," Melinda Chouinard explains in a deadpan, although the results are quite astonishing.

The walls were made from chunks of concrete sidewalk (sometimes called 'urbanite'), hauled in by truck and hand-hewn on site into stone-like masonry. "The challenge with a wall system like this is concrete's low insulation value," said Boise-Cossart. "We insulated sections of the wall with Air Krete, a cementitious foam, which was then plastered. By alternating the plastered wall sections on the interior and exterior, we were able to feature the masonry work on both sides of the building."

Salvaged bridge beams were used for headers and in the timber roof trusses. A blacksmith, Yvon lent his skills by forging tension rods for the trusses. Roof planks were salvaged, as were roof tiles; the latter were augmented by extras from a Roanoke, Texas, company called Tile Search. Broken roofing slates were patterned into a mosaic floor. Cabinetry was fashioned from salvaged and reclaimed California woods of a variety of species, creating a warm, eclectic, artisan aesthetic. Doors, windows, and headers were made from locally salvaged bridge timbers. A picket fence was resurrected from a crumbling churchyard.

Reusing materials does not necessarily result in money savings, and the Chouinard project could not be replicated on a tight budget without the involvement of owner labor and/or a committed team of extremely fit volunteers. It is, however, a testament to the ethic of reuse and perception of value in the waste stream. For Boise-Cossart, the challenge to find recycled materials and develop strategies for resourcefulness was extremely satisfying.

The house is encircled by a tight cluster of garden walls, cisterns, and a garage built of the same materials, and is designed to encourage as much interaction with the world outside as with the cozy interior spaces. The textures of the thick masonry walls and reclaimed woods project a sense of permanence, a connection with both the past and the present that is timeless even though the house is newly built.

Raised from the Rubble

One of the easiest devices to transform sidewalk slabs into stone-like blocks is the good old-fashioned sledge hammer, according to contractor Kit Boise-Cossart. The floors of the house were patterned with broken slate roof tiles. Both outside and in, smooth stuccoed surfaces alternate with hand-hewn 'urbanite' stone sections. The building's owner forged the tension rods for the roof system. Numerous species of California native woods, such as Coulter Pine and Coast Live Oak, found their way into various elements, from the post-and-beam structure to doors and cabinetry.

THE SYNTHETIC AESTHETIC

As more and more homeowners choose to upgrade properties with habitable landscaping and functional outdoor 'rooms,' the patio and decking market has been exponentially expanding. In the best of all worlds, decking solutions would be local, reused, or sustainable. Environmentally-oriented builders should turn to their own regions for appropriate materials or approaches. Many people are choosing options other than decks to satisfy the need for outdoor living spaces. Concrete, brick, earth, stone, and many other materials can be used instead of wooden structures, which typically require regular maintenance and can be relatively short-lived. (Planting native trees and wildlife habitat, growing productive gardens, reducing run-off, and minimizing irrigation needs are also important landscaping priorities.)

Cedars, Redwood, and Pine on Deck

Western red cedar, coast redwood, incense cedar, and Eastern red cedar are in great demand for decking and siding. The same tannins that allowed these species to thrive in the temperate rainforest conditions of the Pacific Northwest make them resistant to rot, weather, and insects. An even greater quantity of preservative-treated Southern pine goes mainly toward structural decking applications. Lesser amounts of Port Orford cedar and Alaskan yellow cedar grace poolsides, patios, and decks. It should come as no surprise that these conventional materials are under severe scrutiny due to unsustainable logging practices and, in the case of pressure-treated wood, the toxicity of the arsenic- and chromium-based chemicals used to enhance their durability. All of these woods should be avoided whenever possible.

The Composite Options

If synthetic fleece garments (made from recycled soda bottles) pass aesthetic and environmental muster, then alternative decking materials that contain recycled-content plastic should, too. Dozens of companies now offer recycled 'plastic lumber,' either wood-plastic composites or 100 percent plastic. These products are being used for decking, trim, fences, benches, docks, retaining walls, picnic tables, and other landscaping and outdoor features. Carpenters may cringe at these new materials because they're a bit like working with salami and don't have the structural strength of wood; but they are highly serviceable substitutes for non-structural decking members, lasting longer, and eliminating the need for regular retreatment to protect against moisture and sun damage.

Winchester, Virginia-based Trex currently leads the synthetic decking materials market. The company turns wood waste from furniture manufacturing shops into sawdust before mixing it in a slurry of plastic resins made from recycled grocery bags and stretch films. The mixture, 50 percent wood and 50 percent recycled plastic, creates a smooth, solid board that weathers to a driftwood grey with subtle variations. According to *Natural Home* magazine, Trex diverted about 90 million pounds of plastic from the waste stream into the decking market in 1999.[3]

Rising from the rolling hills around Junction, Texas, is a mountain of red cedar chips, the byproduct of a perfume

Structural Matters

Non-structural composite decking materials require 16-inch joist spacing, and use more structural members than conventional wooden decks. Many installers prefer systems that facilitate fastening from below, so screw holes are not exposed to view or weather. This deck used a combination of salvaged redwood, ChoiceDek and ACQ-treated lumber.

industry underway in the region since the mid-1940s. Advanced Environmental Recycling Technology, Inc. (AERT) combines long wood fibers from these cedar chips with an engineered blend of recovered plastics including ground-up milk jugs, hard-to-recycle protective inner coatings of beverage cartons, and other high- and low-density polyethylene materials. The resulting goop is extruded into bottom-grooved planks called ChoiceDek, a reddish brown, fairly lightweight material with a gritty surface that fades to a uniform weathered grey. The recovered wood fibers add tensile strength to the plastic resins that hold the material together.

ChoiceDek, Trex, and similar products are guaranteed to last 20 years, although there's no track record to say they won't last longer—or a shorter time for that matter.

There are some legitimate concerns about recycled plastic products. First is our conventional food and agriculture system, in which the average food item travels more than 1,300 miles before arriving at the kitchen table, sometimes requiring a host of preservative treatments along with myriad plastic packaging materials that create waste problems throughout their short lives. Secondly, particularly with mixed-plastic products, there are no systems in place to recycle scraps or whole planks once the useful life of the deck has passed. Then there's the long-term question of how long supplies of cheap petroleum will hold out (although there are probably enough landfilled plastics for mining well into this century). These environmental costs, however, should be weighed against the lifespan of the material, which is expected to be considerably longer than the solid wood it replaces.

Some products presently contain quantities of paper, metal, agricultural residues, and rubber tires. In the future we can expect to see further developments in this family of products—ideally, with increasing emphasis on the use of agricultural fibers, and on improved weight, aesthetics, and durability.

FSC-certified and ACQ-treated Wood

FSC-certified or recovered lumber is often a viable option for structural posts and joists, and for people who really want wood decking planks. In addition to redwood and cedar, other durable though lesser known species, such as elm, are currently being offered at competitive prices. Certified redwood fetches a five percent premium over non-certified. Other exotic FSC-certified exotic woods can cost two to three times more but last three to four times longer than redwood. In addition, lumber pressure-treated with alkaline copper quat (ACQ®) is available for structural deck members as well as for mudsills, and other sensitive uses. ACQ replaces the more toxic ammoniacal copper arsenate (ACA) and chromated copper arsenate (CCA) pressure-treating preservatives. ACQ-treated lumber is durable, contains no EPA classified hazardous chemicals, and can be disposed of in ordinary trash collection.

YESTERDAY'S NEWS, TOMORROW'S BUILDINGS

While paper, in the form of cardboard packaging, blue-prints, and invoices, is abundant on any jobsite, it is increasingly making its way into the finished product as well—the building itself. Cellulose insulation (recycled newspapers) is blown into wall, floor, and ceiling cavities. Pressed paperboard serves as an acoustical buffer, carpet underlayment, and even an exterior wall sheathing. In Japan, concrete forms made from recycled paper are replacing plywood and other tropical woods. Recycled paper facings are becoming standard on products such as gypsum board. A re-emerging technology, known as papercrete or fibrous cement, involves blending shredded waste paper with cement to form lightweight concrete. Taking their lead from Formica™, which contains up to 80 percent recycled paper, other companies are starting to make innovative surfaces for countertops with post-consumer content. Sludge from paper mills, which is typically incinerated or landfilled, is being experimented with to add fiber strength to concrete blocks or slabs. These trends, along with a radically transformed paper industry that dramatically increases the recycled and ag residue content of papers and dramatically reduces the amount of virgin non-FSC-certified materials, point the way toward a more hopeful future for forests.

Paper Stone?

In the Midwest, professor, farmer, and artist Stanley Shetka delved into the world of recycled paper building materials during the course of a conceptual art installation. "I built a kinetic sculpture in which the observer put in waste paper on one end and blocks came out the other side," says Shetka, now president of All Paper Recycling in New Prague, Minnesota. Some of those blocks have weathered the formidable northern climate for over a decade and, since then, Shetka has reportedly constructed, recycled, and remade chairs from paper board as many as 20 times.

Among Shetka's building products is a "tree-free wood" with a class A fire rating, made using a bonding process similar to that in conventional papermaking. He's experimented with all kinds of alternative fibers as well, including kenaf, grass, sunflower seed hulls, rice hulls, and shredded currency. "Clay coated papers have excellent water resistant properties," Shetka notes.

Papercrete or Paper Adobe

Papercrete, or fibrous cement, is made by blending shredded waste paper with sand and cement (and sometimes clay), then using the mixture to produce blocks or monolithic wall systems.

Though still relatively obscure, papercrete is a material upon which proponents can't pile enough accolades: lightweight, structural, highly insulating, sound-absorbing, endlessly recyclable, low-cost, resource-efficient, and aesthetically pleasing, among others.

Papercrete buildings and domes have been erected both from bricks and from pouring the mixture into forms like conventional monolithic concrete. It has been used as mortar material in cordwood construction and as an insulating stucco over earth-bag domes. According to papercrete builder Mike McCain, it also has a good potential for roofs and interior walls, and as an insulative subfloor beneath radiant-heated slabs.

Papercrete, however, exhibits a number of quirky characteristics. Among them is that the material dries very slowly, shrinking and leaving pockets of air. These pockets can then reabsorb water throughout the building's life cycle. There is also limited information on papercrete, despite decades of experimentation since it was patented in the late 1920s.

Eric Patterson, a New Mexico printer, began experimenting with papercrete more than a decade ago in the interest of doing something with excess paper. He built a number of structures—still standing and in good operating condition—that he claims to be ten times more energy-efficient than adobe. Patterson is convinced that it will take a large company to develop the technology and work out building code issues to bring it to the mainstream.

"Somebody one day is going to make a fortune from this process," Patterson insists. "They'll have to develop a method of making consistent blocks that are milled to precise specifications, then glued or mortared in place."

Post-consumer Columns

Standard kraft tubing, which commonly makes its way into landfills, has been used to substitute for table legs by workstation manufacturer StudioEg, in Emeryville, California. Japanese architect Shigeru Ban has been developing some high-profile examples of structural and load-bearing elements made entirely of cardboard cylinders. Ban designed a pavilion for the Hanover 2000 exhibit, and has been working to improve the material's resistance to water, fire, and other hazards. In *Grow Your Own House*, author Jean Dethier explains: "Using this mastery of this innovative and reliable building system ... Ban designed a pavilion of serene elegance. The curves and counter-curves of the cardboard structure (tubes 12 cm in diameter and 25 mm thick) also frame a truly poetic landscape. The whole of this remarkable project was designed to develop an industrial recycling process capable of being widely extended to other eco-progressive buildings."[4]

Rolling With It

Japanese architect Shigeru Ban is fundamentally a scrounger interested in using overlooked, ubiquitous materials for architectural applications, says Dana Buntrock, professor of architecture at the University of California at Berkeley. These photos, taken by Buntrock, are from the Galerie MDS in Tokyo.

One of Ban's most impressive installations is his pavilion designed for the Hanover 2000 expo, made primarily from the cardboard tubes used to roll fabric on—of which there is no shortage. With collaboration between designers and roll manufacturers, the lives of these materials could be extended well beyond their typical short-term use.

Benefits: Straw and other agricultural residues are a natural 'waste' product. Using ag residues to create building products, rather than burning or composting them, can reduce greenhouse gas emissions. Ag residues have good structural fiber characteristics. Compressed straw panels can have an R-value of 1.8 per inch. Holds the potential for mini-mills and regional building systems. Binding adhesives for ag residues tend to be less toxic and more moisture-resistant than adhesives for wood fibers. Excellent machinability. Lighter in weight than wood particleboard. Distinctive, pleasant smell. More visual character than conventional panelboards.

Challenges: Monocrop production of wheat, soy beans, rice, corn, and other crops can be environmentally damaging to soil, watersheds, and wildlife. Companies have had a difficult time breaking into wood-based panel industries, which enjoy economies of scale and cheap sources of fiber. Some panels are based on metric units rather than the U.S. standard four-by-eight-foot module. Transportation costs from the manufacturing facility can play a key role in cost effectiveness.

Applications: Surface finishes. Some structural, wall, and sheathing applications. Core material for laminated doors, paneling, and other products.

Burning Issue

Straw burning is an annual agricultural activity in farm fields across North America. According to Environmental Building News, *using just 25 percent of the available straw could provide exterior walls for 2.7 million 1,000-square-foot buildings each year.*

BUILDING WITH THE GRAIN

Every year in farm fields across North America, millions of tons of agricultural residues, the fibrous castaways of food production—straw, stems, and seed hulls—are burned, left to rot, or assigned to some other undervalued fate. Fiber crops like industrial hemp, kenaf, flax, and others, that can play valuable roles in crop rotation, are in short supply. However, thanks to deforestation, overconsumption, economic globalization, overproduction of certain commodity crops, degraded air quality, and other factors, 'ag' fibers are gaining a bit of popularity. Wheat, rice, rye grass, soybean straw, bagasse, corn stalks, hemp, kenaf, rice hulls, flax shives, sunflower stalks, and seed hulls are just a few of the many agricultural fibers finding their way into building and furniture materials in low-density insulation boards, medium-density fiberboards, hardboards, particleboards, shingles, and other composite products.

Using these fibers to manufacture products, in the place of wood, can mean more forest left intact and less carbon dioxide generated. It is clear from a decade of pioneering business start-ups, however, that a number of factors determine the ability of a region's agricultural fibers to compete with wood: the distance between farm fields and manufacturing facilities (and, therefore, transportation costs); the fiber yield, available harvest, and storage capabilities; and the need for specialized processing and manufacturing machinery based on the particular characteristics of ag fibers rather than wood.

The fact that agricultural fibers are farmed rather than extracted from forests, and can be considered waste products rather than virgin materials, however, doesn't mean they are without impacts. Industrial agriculture's chemical- and machine-intensive, monocrop production methods have been, and continue to be, among humankind's most ecologically destructive practices, and the conversion of forests and other wildlands to farm fields is one of the greatest threats to biodiversity. As Tracy Mumma points out very concisely in the *Guide to Resource Efficient Building Elements*, "In order for agricultural fibers to provide a long-term, resource-efficient building material supply, agriculture must be conducted in a resource-efficient manner that allows for long-term stewardship of the soil. Practices such as crop rotation, cover cropping, and organic farming all contribute to the viability of long-term cultivation and fiber utilization."[5]

Farm-Grown Housing

Notwithstanding the catalyzing role of straw-bale construction in the natural building revival, many experts believe that straw's greatest contribution to the construction industry may eventually come in the form of industrial panels. According to the *Alternate Panel Report*, for example, worldwide demand for panelboard will increase 38 percent over the next decade, requiring an additional 57 million cubic meters of panel products annually.[6]

Environmental Building News offered a number of scenarios describing the potential implications of using 25 percent (35 million tons) of the available straw harvest for the building industry, based on statistics between 1987 and 1994. "If we used all of the available straw for the exterior walls of straw-bale buildings, 2.7 million 1,000-square-foot single-story houses could be built each year. If we turned

that straw into structural compressed straw panels, they could provide the exterior walls, roofs, interior partition walls, and floors of 1 million 2,000-square-foot two-story houses per year. Or, that straw could be used to produce 22 billion square feet of 3/4-inch particleboard, which is five times the current United States production of particleboard and medium-density fiberboard (all thicknesses)."[7]

Meeting the Challenge of the Market

The holy grail of building applications for agricultural fibers lies in the development of regional mills that can produce panelboard products as well as agriculturally based structural insulated panels. Such mini-mills would be located close to farming areas and serve, first and foremost, the surrounding regional markets. California's Sacramento Valley rice-growing region, the grain belt of the Midwest, and the sugar cane production corridors of the Southeast are all examples of areas with ample supply of both raw materials and customers. In this scenario, the benefits of using straw would be available to many who don't have the time, luxury, or ability to construct their own straw-bale homes. Unfortunately, a number of early attempts to establish alter-

Field Planks

The range of agricultural fiber panels seems to vary widely, from those that resemble particleboard to less processed products, such as this one, made in Australia and supplied to us by Van der Ryn Architects. For an extensive list of materials, see pages 118-119 and 129-130.

native structural fiber companies in the United States have been plagued by poor marketing, excessive start-up costs, and other problems. This underscores the difficulty—despite using a very cheap resource like straw—in challenging the wood products industry.

Nearly a dozen mills have been or are being established across North America's grain belt to convert wheat and rice straw, bagasse (sugar cane residue), soy straw, and fiber crops into panelboards. Within the next decade, it appears that significant attempts will be made to penetrate the wood-based panel market with ag fibers, and because they hold a number of performance and environmental advantages, a wide range of new products should come into the main-stream. 'Straw composite panels' which include medium density fiberboard (MDF), particleboard, and hardboard are generally used for interior applications such as counters, trims, moldings, furniture, and cabinetry. 'Structural panels' (typically plywood and OSB) are used for exterior sheathing, subflooring, concrete forming, and exterior signs and fixtures. Oriented straw strand board (the author's term) should be available as a structural panel in the future. Also on the frontier are structural insulated panels that use straw either as the insulating core medium or outer skins or both.

The Ties that Bind

Among the major differences between wood-based and ag fiber-based panels is the chemical used to fuse the fibers together. Many wood-based products still use urea- or phenol-formaldehyde resins that can off-gas a suspected car-cinogen. Formaldehyde resins don't work well with most agricultural fibers, however, because of the fibers' waxy surface. Instead, a polymeric diphenylmethane diisocyante (PMDI) binder is usually used. This is a petroleum-based product used commonly to produce rigid foam for products such as car seating, soft furnishings, and shoe soles. There are questions about the recyclability of fibers bound together with PMDI resin. According to a Dow Chemical scientist, another significant concern is that PMDI has to be handled very carefully throughout the production process. "You don't want to touch it or breathe it. Once set in the board, however, the resin remains stable and safe for consumers." Incidentally, Dow Chemical Company, a leading supplier of PMDI resin, also owns a stake in North America's leading straw panel-board manufacturer, Isobord Enterprises. As this book goes to press, numerous companies and research organizations are working on water-resistant, soy protein-based resins to replace both formaldehyde and PMDI resins and be applicable for wood composite products as well as ag fibers.

A number of new panel products use finely chopped particles of wheat straw to create a smoother, more uniform finish than particleboard with attractive gold, brown, and silver high-lights. At least one product, Meadowboard, manufactured in Albany, Oregon, features a more handcrafted and less indus-trial character. Meadowboard is made by compressing whole stalks of rye straw into a uniquely textured surface that weaves entire plant shafts together in a pattern. One of numerous positive attributes of these agricultural panel-boards is their smell: instead of off-gassing toxic chemicals, they often project a pleasant cereal-like odor.

Load-Bearing Straw Panels

The concept of making 'compressed agricultural fiber' (CAF)

panels was invented in Sweden in 1935 by Theodore Dieden and later developed commercially in Britain by Torsten Mossesson in the late 1940s under the name Stramit. This technology presses straw into a strong continuous membrane using high heat and the fibers' natural binders. The result is a resilient, bale-like panel, two to four inches thick, which is later faced with kraft paper. Most CAF systems have pre-routed channels for wiring and a fastening mechanism to hold them securely together. With the original patents on CAF technology now expired, numerous Stramit manufacturers have emerged in several European countries and Australia. Stramit Industries, Ltd., has reported over 250,000 buildings being erected using these panels in the United Kingdom.[8] Efforts to develop a production infrastructure in the United States have been short-lived and many builders pine for the reappearance of straw panels that could be used in a vast number of building applications.

This is an infant industry with many different players. At least seven mills were operating in North America as of January 2000 (see list on pages 129-130) with 12 more planned or proposed in the near future. With grain prices at all-time lows, the agriculture industry is clearly looking for new outlets for its products and ways for farmers to earn more. For the short-term, however, the greatest advances in small-scale compressed structural straw panel systems will probably be made in developing countries, where the need for new technologies is urgent and the market potential is huge.

Currently, global demand for household and office furniture—fueled by favorable 'free trade' incentives—represents the largest market for particleboard and medium-density fiberboard. While the beauty of using agricultural residues lies in regional applications in the context of a sustainable future, the current trend seems to be toward establishing highly capital-intensive mills designed to compete head-on with the wood products industry, producing hundreds of tons of material per day for export use. There is still hope, however, that one day every region will have its own range of distinctive building materials, in which agricultural fibers may play a leading part.

Strawboard Wall Finish

Strawboard provides an alternative to sheetrock for walls, ceilings, and other applications. The surfaces can then be painted, stained, sealed, or left unfinished. These photos show Isobord as wall and ceiling surfaces in this functional building.

Look around any house, apartment, or office building and you'll find interior partitions, flooring and counter surfaces, siding and sheathing, roofing and other applications that present ideal opportunities for FSC-certified, recycled, and non-wood materials.

By mining materials from the waste stream—industrial, municipal, urban, and agricultural—panelboards, tiles, custom counters, shakes, and dozens of other value-added products are being created. Some are economically competitive and hold the promise of mass distribution. Others are strictly high-end, and are deservedly so because of the labor-intensive and artisanal nature of their fabrication, or because of the realities of start-up industries.

Consider the following samples as just the foundation of a materials library that should be regularly updated (with regional emphasis) and that can be supplemented and further researched with the resources listed at the end of this section.

FSC On Board

The Forest Stewardship Council (FSC) currently represents the only environmentally credible program to promote more ecologically-based forestry. Still in its infancy, the FSC attempts to ensure that certified companies adopt long-term management policies that protect watersheds, native biodiversity, and local cultures in addition to providing renewable materials. The United States' FSC program is competing, however, with the American Forest & Paper Association's Sustainable Forestry Initiative (SFI), an industry-sponsored, voluntary program with significantly lower (and optional) standards. FSC-certified wood options are rapidly expanding, while the availability of FSC-certified board products, like particleboard from Collins Pine and interior plywood from Columbia Forest Products, is currently limited. (www.collinspine.com; www.columbiaforestproducts.com; www.certifiedwood.org)

FSC-Certified California Chestnut Oak Floors

Mendocino Redwood Company, FSC-certified in late 2000, has accomplished what many have tried for decades to achieve. Their line of California Chestnut oak (a.k.a.tanoak) flooring makes use of an aggressive hardwood species that is regularly chipped, incinerated, or sprayed with toxic herbicides. Through a sophisticated drying, milling, and sorting operation, the company transforms an unwanted species (normally sold at a loss) into three grades of quality hardwood flooring. Along the way, raw material use is maximized, and all byproducts are used or recycled.

(www.mrc.com)

Prefinished FSC Particleboard

Eco Colors, offered by Architectural Forest Enterprises (Vida) in Brisbane, California, come in a variety of UV-cured finishes for cabinetry, wall panel, and other finish applications.

(www.4vida.com)

Finger Joints

Post-industrial scrap wood can be re-milled and finger-jointed to produce new studs. Finger-jointed lumber is often wrapped with veneers to produce trims, moldings, stiles, and door jambs. Contact Lumber in Portland, Oregon, is one supplier of these products.

(www.contactlumber.com)

Post-industrial Parquet

The Oregon Lumber Company recovers short scraps and cut-offs from door makers and manufacturers in the Portland area and 'up-cycles' them into an innovative flooring product called Worthwood. The individual blocks are placed on end, and arranged via a soft wire to make strips of flooring material. Using the end grain takes advantage of an extremely porous surface that absorbs resins and colors very effectively. The result is a resilient, long-lasting floor surface that requires far less maintenance than conventional plank and parquet materials and is easily cut and sanded with conventional carpentry tools. Oregon Lumber's source material is recovered, but not FSC-certified, and company president John Couch modestly describes it as "tinged green."

(www.oregonlumber.com)

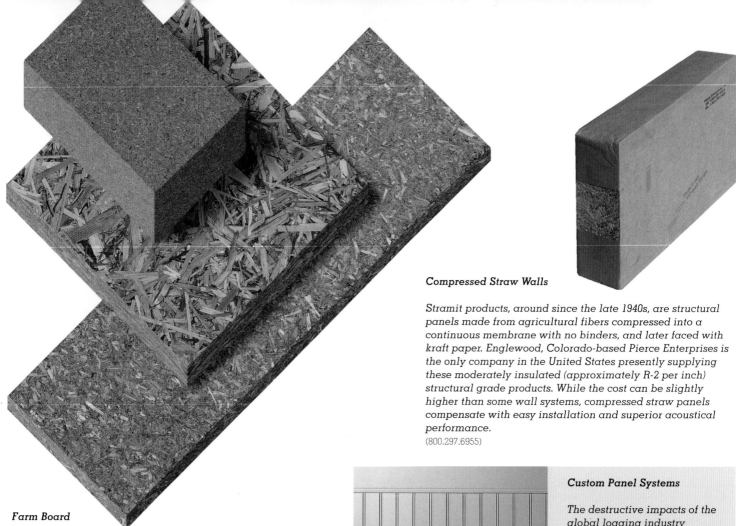

Compressed Straw Walls

Stramit products, around since the late 1940s, are structural panels made from agricultural fibers compressed into a continuous membrane with no binders, and later faced with kraft paper. Englewood, Colorado-based Pierce Enterprises is the only company in the United States presently supplying these moderately insulated (approximately R-2 per inch) structural grade products. While the cost can be slightly higher than some wall systems, compressed straw panels compensate with easy installation and superior acoustical performance.
(800.297.6955)

Farm Board

A number of companies are producing wood-free particleboard and other non-structural and structural panel products from row crop 'waste.' Straw is the primary feedstock for these formaldehyde-free products, though bagasse (sugar cane pulp) is used in warmer regions of the country as well. Most of the ag fiber boards find their way into cabinetry and other non-structural applications, an industry segment expected to grow exponentially over the next decade.

Custom Panel Systems

The destructive impacts of the global logging industry inspired New England Classic's founder John Crowley to develop ways to use fibers as effectively as possible. Based in Portland, Maine, the company makes a variety of paneling systems that innovatively combine recycled wood or wheat straw panelboards (often formaldehyde-free) as the primary core material, with veneers or other decorative surfaces.
(www.newenglandclassic.com)

21st Century Plastics

Biocomposites, which couple waste plastics with agricultural fibers such as hemp, kenaf, or flax, are among the many emerging alternatives to products typically manufactured from wood dust. Teel Global Resource Technologies of Madison, Wisconsin, is producing a range of such materials aimed at improving the aesthetics, durability, and strength-to-weight ratio of current composite plastics. The shakes are made from recycled plastic milk jugs and various natural fibers. The material samples at left are combinations of recycled plastics, jute, sisal, coconut, and kenaf.

(608.232.9432)

Straw, Soybeans, and Sunflower Seeds

They sometimes look like stone, burl, or just plain particleboard, but in fact they are amalgams of recycled newsprint and agricultural wastes like sunflower seed hulls, and soybean and wheat straw. One of the most successful projects to emerge from the now-defunct USDA Alternative Agriculture Research and Commercialization Cooperative program to expand uses for agricultural crops, Mankato, Minnesota-based Phenix Biocomposites makes specialty particleboard products, including faux-finish, high-end surface boards. In late 2000, Phenix gained approval for structural grade wheat and soybean straw board, which the company claims will be cost-competitive with OSB.

(www.phenixbiocomposites.com)

Synthetic Decking

According to the California Redwood Association, some 3 million new decks are produced every year. Non-structural composite materials combining recycled plastics and wood fibers (also frequently recycled) are becoming increasingly common. In the case of ChoiceDek (above), high-and-low density waste plastics are blended with waste cedar chips, byproducts of the perfume industry.

Trex, (bench detail), is another popular option.

 For structural materials, consider ACQ® Preserve treated lumber, which contains no arsenic, chromium or other EPA classified hazardous chemicals, unlilke conventional pressure treated lumber.

Metal fastening systems, such as Deckmaster, allow studs to be attached to the joists from below, hiding screw connections from view and protecting them from the elements.

(See www.treatedlumber.com for more information on ACQ).

Grass Floors

Bamboo is the world's fastest and tallest growing grass and in many regions of the world is heavily depended upon for construction materials (in addition to food, clothing, and paper).

Tongue and groove bamboo plywood flooring products are available from numerous suppliers. The extremely durable bamboo is imported— harvesting conditions and binder materials should be checked out with suppliers in advance.

Heavy Duty Metal

Until recently, used only in the commercial building world, high recycled-content steel is making its way into the green building vocabulary. At the Post Ranch Inn in Big Sur, California, steel is used on doors and roofs.

Inside and Out

Metal roofing materials can double as siding. It's long-lasting and most probably has a recycled content. At the Apple Farm guest houses in Philo, California, metal siding is used inside and out—on roofs, siding, and even on an interior ceiling, all to nice effect.

Junk Mail Construction

Louise and Bill Pape of Los Ojos, New Mexico, have embarked on a number of natural building projects, including this chicken coop made from papercrete. Papercrete is a mixture of shredded recycled paper, cement, sand, and water. Scraps can be thrown back into the portable mixer.

Post-consumer ply

Simplex Products in Adrian, Michigan, produces thin but remarkably strong panels of 100 percent recycled paper waste (80 percent post-consumer content) that offer superior racking and shear strength and energy efficiency advantages.
(www.ludlowcp.com)

Recovered Gypsum

An increasing number of synthetic gypsum products on the market are made from the reclaimed emissions and byproducts of manufacturing and energy production.
Recycled scrap wallboard is used as well. Most wallboard facings are made from either 100 percent post-consumer recycled newspapers or old corrugated containers.
(www.usg.com)

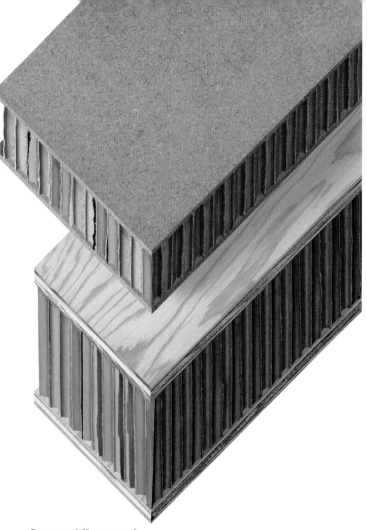

Structural Honeycomb

The technology used to produce kraft paper honeycomb panels has been around for a few decades. Entire houses reportedly have been erected from such panels in an experimental development project. Today, honeycomb panels are primarily used as lightweight portable floors, walls, and roof panels for the trade show industry. According to Steve Loudin of Tricel in Gurnee, Illinois, honeycomb's dead air space traps sound and provides a strength-to-weight ratio greater than plywood. Wood veneered structural panels for floor systems would require virgin fibers; non-structural panels can be made from post-consumer waste.

(www.tricelcorp.com)

Paper Panels

Every day in northwestern New Jersey, between 150 and 200 tons of newspapers are turned into sound-deadening acoustical fiberboards, packaging, and other products at the Homasote manufacturing facility. The (non-deinked) newspaper fibers are bound together with a wax emulsion to produce egg carton-like grey boards in a variety of thicknesses and densities. As a resilient, highly insulative carpet underlayment system, Homasote board competes with a combination gypcrete and plywood subfloor system. Another Homasote product is being used as a structural roofing panel. Because it's remarkably weather-resistant, the paperboard also has potential for sheathing. Cork-faced office partitions are one of the company's top-sellers.

(www.homasote.com)

40-Year Floors

Linoleum is an enduring finish surface manufactured from a number of natural, renewable ingredients. According to the Center for Resourceful Building Technology, linoleum is often referred to as a "40-year floor." It begins with linseed oil, a product of flax, and natural resins to which cork powder, wood flour, and limestone are added. It can be used on floors, countertops, desks, and other work surfaces without sacrificing indoor air quality.
(www.flexco.com)

Rubber Slate

Related to walkway pads that have weathered on docks for 30 years, these slate-like shingles are made from 100% recovered post-industrial plastic and rubber scrap, primarily cast-asides from the automotive industry. When applied by an approved contractor, they have a 50-year warranty.
(www.ecostarinc.com)

Malleable Marble

Linoleum also comes in a wide range of colors and marblized patterns. Marmoleum, imported by Forbo North America, is a malleable and colorful material that can be an excellent choice for flooring, countertops, and other surfaces.
(www.forbo-industries.com)

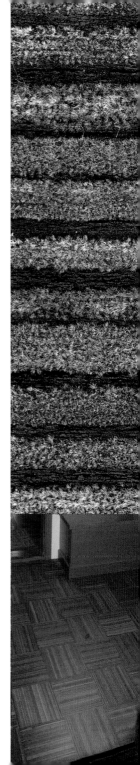

Re-tirement

Perhaps the most high-profile use of tires in residential construction has been the Earthship, pioneered by Michael Reynolds and popularized by Dennis Weaver. Outside of Taos, New Mexico, an entire development of earthships is dug into the ground. Their greenhouse glazing can be seen glimmering like mirrors across the sagebrush landscape. This building, designed by Cornell University architecture professor John Shaw, incorporates some of the principles of earthships, such as the rammed earth/tire walls.

Recycled Composite Shakes

These shakes combine post-industrial scraps from the medical industry with recycled wood pallets and other recovered wood fibers to produce long-lasting, UV-protected wood shingle alternatives.
(www.ecoshake.com)

Heavy Traffic

Even without the now infamous Firestone recall, tires have been a solid waste problem in the United States to the tune of a quarter million per year. Using recycled tire materials can offer many constructive opportunities. Flooring tiles and matting rolls can be used in high traffic areas, such as mud rooms, retail stores, entryways, and other public spaces.
(www.regupol.com) (above)
(www.flexco.com) (right)

Righteous Details

An increasing number of manufacturers offer architectural tiles made partially or entirely from recycled glass. Among them are Bedrock Industries from Seattle, Washington (the small square on left) and Aurora Glass in Eugene, Oregon (all others pictured above). Brian Haldane of the St. Vincent de Paul Society in Eugene, Oregon, had no experience with glass recycling before starting the Society's Aurora Glass project. Teaming up with a local agency that recycles deconstruction materials, he learned to make architectural tiles using decommissioned windows as a primary feedstock. "Old single-pane window glass has little value with present energy efficiency demands for glazing," says Haldane. "By converting the glass into tiles and other things, we're using deconstruction materials to make brand new building products." The rosette blocks and drawer pulls are made of 100 percent recycled materials and come in a palette of vibrant retro colors. Manufacturing blocks provides jobs, and profits go toward helping the homeless and low-income people. Tiles and blocks also go into low-income housing projects St. Vincent de Paul develops.

Bedrock Industries, 206.283.0497 (www.bedrockindustries.com)
Aurora Glass, 888.291.9311 (www.aurora-glass.com)

Walls of Empties

Landscapes are littered with inspired but half-finished bottle and mortar construction projects. When executed properly, the results can be quite stunning.

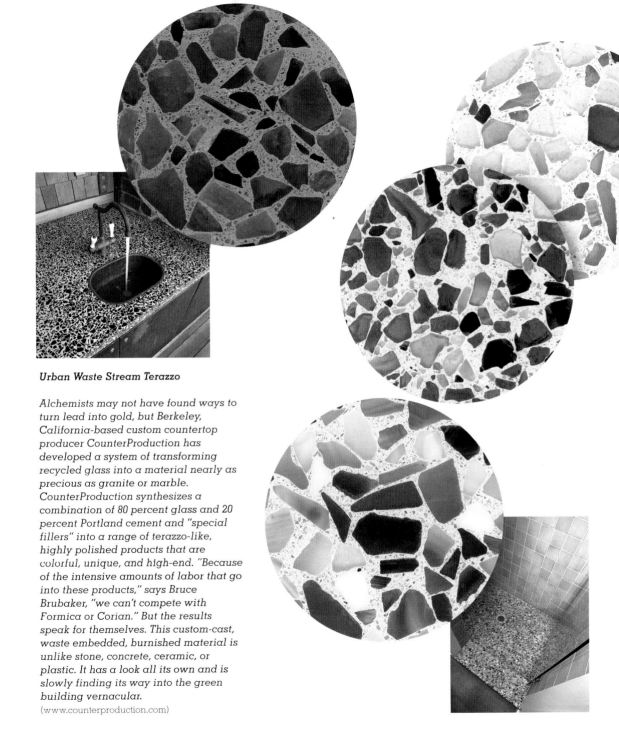

Urban Waste Stream Terazzo

Alchemists may not have found ways to turn lead into gold, but Berkeley, California-based custom countertop producer CounterProduction has developed a system of transforming recycled glass into a material nearly as precious as granite or marble. CounterProduction synthesizes a combination of 80 percent glass and 20 percent Portland cement and "special fillers" into a range of terazzo-like, highly polished products that are colorful, unique, and high-end. "Because of the intensive amounts of labor that go into these products," says Bruce Brubaker, "we can't compete with Formica or Corian." But the results speak for themselves. This custom-cast, waste embedded, burnished material is unlike stone, concrete, ceramic, or plastic. It has a look all its own and is slowly finding its way into the green building vernacular.

(www.counterproduction.com)

Syndecrete Surfaces

Perhaps no one knows the custom pre-cast lightweight concrete business better than David Hertz, an architect who founded Santa Monica, California-based Syndecrete in the mid-1980s. "Cement can be used in nearly every building application," says Hertz, "from garden walls to floors, wall tiles, doors, countertops, and furniture."

Cement, like aluminum and steel, requires a great deal of energy in its initial production. This can be mitigated, however, by reducing the amount of cement in the mix with substitutes from the waste stream. Waste material from fly ash to bottle glass to carpet fibers can be captured in the mix. For the Metreon store in San Francisco, Hertz embedded 15,000 pounds of Sony electronics cast-offs into a panel. He has cast watch parts in cement slabs for Swatch, and zippers, snaps, and other accessories in a project for the Patagonia sportswear company as well. Hertz's home in Venice, California, is a monument to Syndecrete. Stone-like cement meets fir meets steel in an open breezy design that uses concrete in sophisticated applications. A Syndecrete pass-through wall ties the entire space together and also appears in the form of floors, countertops, showers, sinks, fireplaces—even couches.

(www.syndesisinc.com)

Urbanite

Torn-up sidewalks can provide materials for various applications, like this garden wall in Tesuque, New Mexico. Contractor Kit Boise-Cossart, who built the Chouinard house featured on page 106, reports that a sledge hammer is the best tool for making blocks.

Fiber-Cement Siding

Fiber-cement hardboard products from companies such as ABT, Eternit, and James Hardie are becoming increasingly common alternatives to solidwood siding, trim, and roofing. Most products can be cut and drilled with conventional hand tools and applied directly to wood or steel studs up to 24 inches on center.
Some fiber-cement products come with up to 50-year guarantees. Most of the wood fibers are imported.

Consider these high recycled content resources as a starting point for suppliers of wall paneling (some structural products are available), shelving, cabinetry, countertops, flooring and underlayments, shingles, trim and other finish materials. These resources are in continual flux and the best sources of current information are databases that are regularly updated, such as those of the Center for Resourceful Building Technologies (www.crbt.org), Environmental Building News (www.buildinggreen.com), Architects/Designers/ Planners for Social Responsibility–Northern California chapter (CD-Rom) and the Harris Directory (www.harrisdirectory.com). The information centers listed also keep up with this rapidly evolving field. Search out regional suppliers and contact local home improvement and hardware stores for innovative products.

Agricultural Product Suppliers

ALL PAPER RECYCLING
New Prague, Minnesota
952.758.6577
Shetka Stone and other tree-free panelboard products.

ARCHITECTURAL FOREST ENTERPRISES
Brisbane, California
800.483.6337/415.467.4800
www.4vida.com
Colored non-wood panels and FSC-certified panels for furniture, door cores, and more.

BIOFAB/PACIFIC GOLD BOARD
Redding, California
530.243.4032/2341
www.strawboard.com
info@ricestraw.com
Wheat and rice straw panelboard products, including interior partitions and acoustical panels.

CALIFORNIA AGRIBOARD, LLC
Willows, California
530.742.1846
MDF rice straw facility, to be up and running in the future.

COMPAK SYSTEMS
Lincolnshire, England
44 (0) 1427 616927
www.compaksystems.com
Formaldehyde-free ag fiber panels with numerous production facilities worldwide.

FIBERTECH
Colusa, California
530.458.4547
Rice straw particleboard for cabinets, floor underlayment, and other non-structural applications.

HAWAIIAN DURAGREEN
780.458.1007
www.panelsource.net
Particleboard and other products made from bagasse (sugar cane residue).

ISOBORD
Portland, Oregon
503.242.7345
www.isobordenterprises.com
Largest supplier of wheat straw panelboard.

MEADOWOOD INDUSTRIES
Albany, Oregon
541.259.1331
www.meadowoodindustries.com
Artisan quality straw panels.

PACIFIC NORTHWEST FIBER
Plummer, Idaho
208.686.6800
877.GO GRAIN (brokers)
www.pacificfiber.com
Particleboard and underlayment panels made from grass seed straw and phenolic resin binder.

PHENIX BIOCOMPOSITES
Mankato, Minnesota
800.324.8187
www.phenixbiocomposites.com
(note: no 'o' in phenix)
Panelboard products including a structural panel made out of wheat and soybean straw, sunflower seed hulls, and other recovered fibers, using formaldehyde-free binder.

PIERCE ENTERPRISES INC.
Englewood, Colorado
800.297.6955
easipierce@mindspring.com
Compressed straw structural panels from 2.25 to 3.5 inches thick; no adhesives used; load-bearing panels available; 3-4 months lead time necessary. More plants planned.

PRAIRIE FOREST PRODUCTS
Hutchinson, Kansas
316.665.7000
prairieforest@mindspring.com
Wheat straw particleboard.

PRIME BOARD
Wahpeton, North Dakota
701.642.9700/701.642.1152
800.wheatbd 9432823
www.primeboard.com
Wheat straw, sunflower hulls, flax shives for furniture and cabinetry applications.

PYRAMOD INTERNATIONAL
Grass Valley, California
530.477.2515
Manufacturing system for modular compressed straw panels, primarily in developing countries.

TEEL-GLOBAL RESOURCE TECHNOLOGIES
Madison, Wisconsin
608.232.9432
grot@execpc.com
Ag fiber-recycled polyethylene composite shingled roof panels.

WESTGRAIN
St. Albert, Alberta, Canada
877.GoGrain
www.panelsource.net
Wheat straw panels.

Engineered Wood Waste-based Panel Products

ADVANCED WOOD RESOURCES
Brownsville, Oregon
800.533.3374
www.comply-awr.com
Comply wood waste panels that are more durable than structural plywood.

CAN FIBER
909.682.8500 California
716.827.3008 New York
416.681.9990 Toronto
www.canfibre.com
100% reclaimed wood from metropolitan waste stream using a phenol formaldehyde binder under the AllGreen label.

SIERRAPINE
Roseville, California
800.676.3339
www.medite.com
Medite MDF products are made from 90% certified pre-consumer wood waste. Some formaldehyde-free products available.

WILLAMETTE INDUSTRIES
Portland, Oregon
541.744.4639
www.wii.com
MDF using 40% urban wood waste.

Wood Trim Products

CONTACT LUMBER
Portland, Oregon
800.824.3296
Finger-jointed core (from post-industrial scrap) with veneer for trim, moldings, and jamb applications.

NEW ENGLAND CLASSIC
Portland, Maine
888.880.6324
207.773.6144
www.homefittings.com
Paneling and trim made from discarded wheat straw, sawdust, or wood pallets with a finished hardwood veneer.

TEMPLE-INLAND FOREST PRODUCTS
Diboll, Texas
800.231.6060
Wood chip-based trim products for interior or exterior applications.

Recycled Paper Boards

HOMASOTE
West Trenton, New Jersey
800.257.9491
www.homasote.com
Recycled newsprint board for acoustical buffers, floor underlayment, exterior sheathing, and other applications.

THERMO-PLY
Adrian, Michigan
800.345.8881/517.263.8881
www.ludlowcp.com
Recycled paper panels with non-permeable foil facing for structural applications.

TRICEL
Gurnee, Illinois
800.352.3300
www.tricelcorp.com
Kraft honeycomb panels with plywood veneers for structural and non-structural applications, primarily for exhibition industry.

Reclaimed Gypsum Board

GEORGIA PACIFIC
Newington, New Hampshire
603.433.8000
www.gp.com/gypsum/index.html
Recovered gypsum drywall for interior walls and ceilings.

US GYPSUM
Fiber Rock
Chicago, Illinois
800.874.4968
www.usg.com
Sheetrock using recycled wood fiber and recovered gypsum.

Agricultural Fiber Information Centers

AGROTECH COMMUNICATIONS
Memphis, Tennessee
901.757.1777
901.309.1668
www.agfibertechnology.com
Organization focused on trends in the ag fibers industry.

ALBERTA RESEARCH COUNCIL
780.450.5411
Leading edge research on ag fiber technology.

ALTERNATIVE PANEL REPORT
St. Albert, Alberta, Canada
780.458.1007
877.GO GRAIN
www.panelsource.net
Newsletter on the alternative panel industry; distributor of numerous alternative panel products.

ASSOCIATION OF BIO-BASED INDUSTRIES
St. Louis, Missouri
608.835.0428
www.newuses.org
New ag fiber trade organization to be working with the USDA New Uses Council.

FIBER FUTURES
San Francisco, California
415.561.6546
www.fiberfutures.org
Non-profit environmental and consulting group for use of agricultural residues and other tree-free fibers in building and other products.

THE HARRIS DIRECTORY
Santa Fe, New Mexico
www.harrisdirectory.com
A great paid resource for recycled building materials.

INSTITUTE FOR LOCAL SELF-RELIANCE
Minneapolis, Minnesota
612.379.3815/202.232.4108
www.ilsr.org/
www.carbohydrateeconomy.org
Promotes use of regional crops for energy and fiber needs.

Floor and Countertop Materials

ECO-SURFACES
Dodge-Regupol
Lancaster, Pennsylvania
877.ECOSURFACES
www.regupol.com
Manufacturer of brightly colored rubber flooring.

FLEX-TUFT
Flexco
Chamblee, Georgia
800.933.3151
www.flexco.com
Manufacturers of rubber entryway tiles and linoleum flooring.

MARMOLEUM
Forbo Industries
Hazleton, Pennsylvania
570.459.0771
800.842.7839
www.forbo-industries.com
Linoleum made from linseed oil, resin, limestone, wood flour, cork flour, pigments, jute.

RECYCLED RUBBER MATTING
McMinnville, Oregon
800.525.5530
www.rbrubber.com
Leader in rubber flooring and rubber recycling technology.

Recycled Glass and Tile Products

AURORA GLASS
Eugene, Oregon
888.291.9311
www.auroraglass.org
Recycled glass tiles, a product of St. Vincent De Paul.

BEDROCK INDUSTRIES
Seattle, Washington
206.283.7625
www.bedrockindustries.com
Recycled glass tile.

TILE SEARCH
Roanoke, Texas
817.491.2444
Source of recycled/reclaimed roofing tiles.

Cast Concrete/Recycled Material Surfaces

SYNDECRETE
Santa Monica, California
310.829.9932
www.syndesisinc.com
Custom cast lightweight concrete with recycled content.

COUNTERPRODUCTION
Berkeley, California
510.843.6916
www.counterproduction.com
Custom terrazzo with recycled content.

SLATESCAPE
Littleton, Colorado
303.978.1199
800.688.8677
www.americanfibercement.com
Economical countertops and work surfaces made from Portland cement and recovered calcium silica (imported from Germany).

NOTES

THE CASE FOR LOCAL SOLUTIONS
1. Tracy Mumma, *Guide to Resource Efficient Building Elements*, 102.
2. Lester Walker, *American Shelter*, 17.
3. Steve Chappell, *The Alternative Building Sourcebook*, 8.
4. "Clearcutting in Your National Forests?" Turning Point Project advertisement, *New York Times*, September 27, 1999.
5 Kathryn Kohm and Jerry Franklin, eds., *Creating a Forestry for the 21st Century*, 3.
6. Thomas Spies, "Forest Stand Structure, Composition, and Function," *Creating a Forestry for the 21st Century*, 12.
7. Tracy Mumma, *Resource Efficient Building Elements*, 106.
8. "Warning—Bioinvasion," Turning Point Project advertisement, *New York Times*, September 20, 1999.
9. Dennis Haldeman, letter to the editor, *Environmental Building News*, July/August 1997.
10. Laurie Wayburn, et. al., *Forest Carbon in the United States: Opportunities and Options for Private Lands*, 16.
11. Ibid.
12. Ibid.
13. Tracy Mumma, *Resource Efficient Building Elements*, 108.

RECYCLED/RECLAIMED/SALVAGED
1. Ann Edminster and Sami Yassa, *Efficient Wood Use in Residential Construction*, 53.
2. Ibid.
3. Scott Lantz and Robert Falk, "Feasibility of Recycling Timber from Military Industrial Buildings," *The Use of Recycled Wood and Paper in Building Applications*, 41.

FRAMING/SIDING/SHEATHING
1. Tracy Mumma, *Guide to Resource Efficient Building Elements*, 16.
2. Steve Loken and Tracy Mumma, "Wood Waste-Based Materials in Building Applications," *The Use of Recycled Wood and Paper in Building Applications*, 7.
3. Steve Chappell, ed., *The Alternative Building Sourcebook for Traditional, Natural and Sustainable Building Products and Services*, 47.
4. David Eisenberg, lecture, Pacific Energy Center, San Francisco, CA, September 13, 2000.

5. "Certified Life-Cycle Impact Profile of North American Steel Production." Study prepared by Scientific Certification Systems Inc., Oakland, California, January 2000.
6. Ibid.
7. Gail Vittori, phone interview by author, December 1, 2000.
8. Steve Chappell, ed., *The Alternative Building Sourcebook*, 47.
9. Jonathan Orpin, "The Use of Salvaged and Resawn Wood in Fine Homebuilding," *The Use of Recycled Wood and Paper in Building Applications*, 101.

INSULATED STRUCTURAL SYSTEMS
1. Kwei Law, Sylvie Rioux, and Jacques Valade, "Wood and paper properties of short rotation poplar clones," *TAPPI Journal* 83, no. 5, May 2000, 1–6.
2. Alex Wilson, "Structural Insulated Panels: An Efficient Way to Build," *Environmental Building News*, May 1998, 10.
3. Tracy Mumma, *Guide to Resource Efficient Building Elements*, 22.

NATURAL BUILDING MOVEMENT
1. David Easton, *The Rammed Earth House*, 111.

RECYCLED MATERIALS AND RESOURCE RECOVERY
1. David Muchnick, "Big City Forest, Inc.: The State-of-the-Art in Value-Added Wood Reclaiming," *Use of Recycled Wood and Paper in Building Applications*, 121.
2. David N.-S. Hon and Wayne Y. Chao, "Commingled Plastic/Rubber/Newsprint Fiber Composites: Their Processability and Physicomechanical Properties," *Recycled Wood and Paper in Building Applications*, 173.
3. Jenny Shortridge, "Decked Out," *Natural Home*, March/April 2000, 76.
4. Jean Dethier, *Grow Your Own House*, 25.
5. Tracy Mumma, *Guide to Resource-Efficient Building Elements*, 105.
6. Panel Source International, "An Overview: The Panelboard Industry," *Alternate Panel Report* 1, no. 1, January 2000, 4.
7. Wilson, Alex, "Straw the Next Great *Building Material?*" *EBN*, May/June 1995, 8.
8. *Ibid*, 6.

BIBLIOGRAPHY AND RECOMMENDED READING

Baker, Paula, Erica Elliott, and John Banta. *PRESCRIPTIONS FOR A HEALTHY HOUSE: A Practical Guide for Architects, Builders, and Homeowners.* Santa Fe, NM: Inword Press, 1998.

Ball, Rick. *Making Space: DESIGN FOR COMPACT LIVING.* Woodstock, NY: The Overlook Press, 1987.

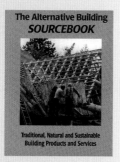

Chappell, Steve, ed., *THE ALTERNATIVE BUILDING SOURCEBOOK: Traditional, Natural and Sustainable Building Products and Services.* Brownfield, ME: Fox Maple Press, 1998.

Clancy-Hepburn, Meghan, Nicole Capretz, and Jay Halfon. *ISSUES IN RESOURCE CONSERVATION.* Washington, D.C.: Resource Conservation Alliance, 1998.

Cusack, Victor. *BAMBOO REDISCOVERED.* Trentham, Victoria: Earth Garden Books, 1997.

Dethier, Jean, et al. *GROW YOUR OWN HOUSE: Simón Vélez and Bamboo Architecture.* Weil am Rhein, Germany: Vitra Design Museum, 2000.

Devall, Bill, ed., *CLEARCUT: the Tragedy of Industrial Forestry.* San Francisco, CA: Sierra Club Books/Earth Island Press, 1993.

Drengson, Alan Rike, and Duncan MacDonald Taylor, eds. *ECOFORESTRY: The Art and Science of Sustainable Forest Use.* Stony Creek, CT: New Society Publishers, 1997.

E Build Library: 1992–1999. AN ENCYCLOPEDIC GREEN BUILDING REFERENCE FROM ENVIRONMENTAL BUILDING NEWS (CD-ROM). Version 3.0, E Build, Inc., 1999.

Easton, David. *THE RAMMED EARTH HOUSE.* White River Junction, VT: Chelsea Green Publishing Company, 1996.

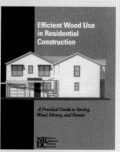

Edminster, Ann, and Sami Yassa. *EFFICIENT WOOD USE IN RESIDENTIAL CONSTRUCTION: A Practical Guide to Saving Wood, Money, and Forests.* New York, NY: National Resources Defense Council, 1998.

Elizabeth, Lynne, and Cassandra Adams, eds., *ALTERNATIVE CONSTRUCTION: Contemporary Natural Building Methods.* New York, NY: John Wiley and Sons, Inc., 2000.

Falk, Robert H., ed., *THE USE OF RECYCLED WOOD AND PAPER IN BUILDING APPLICATIONS.* Madison, WI: Forest Products Society, 1997.

Hellman, Peter. "Green Acres," *METROPOLITAN HOME,* September/October 2000, 88–94.

Holmes, Dwight, Larry Strain, Alex Wilson, and Sandra Leibowitz. *GREEN SPEC: The Environmental Building News Product Directory and Guideline Specifications.* Brattleboro, VT: E Build, Inc., 1999.

Jehl, Douglas. "Logging's Shift South Brings Concern on Oversight," *THE NEW YORK TIMES*, Tuesday, August 8, 2000.

Jenkins, Michael B. and Emily T. Smith. *THE BUSINESS OF SUSTAINABLE FORESTRY: Strategies For An Industry In Transition.* Washington, D.C.: Island Press, 1999.

Karlenzig, Warren, *A BLUEPRINT FOR GREENING AFFORDABLE HOUSING: Developer Guidelines for Resource Efficiency and Sustainable Communities,* Santa Monica, California: Global Green USA, 2000.

Kennedy, Joseph F, ed., *THE ART OF NATURAL BUILDING: Design, Construction, Technology.* Stony Creek, CT: New Society Publishers, 2001.

Kibbey, David, ed., *ADSPR WEST COAST ARCHITECTURAL RESOURCE GUIDE.* Berkeley, CA: Architects/Designers/Planners for Social Responsibility, 1999.

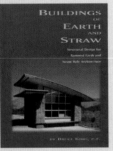

King, Bruce, *BUILDINGS OF EARTH AND STRAW: Structural Design for Rammed Earth and Straw-Bale Architecture.* Sausalito, California: Ecological Design Press, 1996.

Kohm, Kathryn A., and Jerry F. Franklin, eds., *CREATING A FORESTRY FOR THE 21ST CENTURY.* Washington, D.C.: Island Press, 1997.

Laporte, Robert. *MOOSEPRINTS: A Holistic Home Building Guide.* Santa Fe, NM: Natural Home Building Center, 1993.

Leaf, Sue. "Whither Walden?" *UTNE READER,* September/October 1999, 49–52. Originally published in *Architecture Minnesota,* March/April 1999.

Loken, Steve. *RECRAFT 90: The Construction of a Resource Efficient House.* Missoula, MT: Center For Resourceful Building Technology, 1993.

Lotzkar, Ruth, and Ada Brown. *ENVIRONMENTAL INFORMATION TOOLS FOR SUSTAINABLE CONSUMER GUIDE.* Vancouver, BC: Environmentally Sound Packaging Coalition of Canada, 1999.

Lstiburek, Joseph Ph.D. *BUILDER'S GUIDE.* Westford, MA: Building Science Corporation, 2000.

Marinelli, Janet, and Paul Bierman-Lytle. *YOUR NATURAL HOME: The Complete Sourcebook and Design Manual for Creating a Healthy, Beautiful, and Environmentally Sensitive House.* New York, NY: Little, Brown and Company, 1995.

Martin, Glen. "Branching Out," *SAN FRANCISCO CHRONICLE,* Wednesday, August 9, 2000,1(C).

McCain, Mike. *Fibrous Cement: AN ALTERNATIVE BUILDING MATERIAL.* Self-published booklet.

Menotti, Victor. *FREE TRADE, FREE LOGGING: How The World Trade Organization Undermines Global Forest Conservation, A Special Report by the IFG.* San Francisco, CA: International Forum of Globalization, 1999.

Morris, David, and Irshad Ahmed. *THE CARBOHYDRATE ECONOMY: Making Chemicals and Industrial Materials From Plant Matter.* Washington, D.C.: Institute for Local Self-Reliance, 1992.

Mumma, Tracy. *GUIDE TO RESOURCE EFFICIENT BUILDING ELEMENTS,* 6th ed. Missoula, MT: The Center for Resourceful Building Technology, 1997.

Nattrass, Brian, and Mary Altomare. *THE NATURAL STEP FOR BUSINESS: Wealthy Ecology and The Evolutionary Corporation.* Stony Creek, CT: New Society Publishers, 1999.

Pauli, Gunter. *UPSIZING: The Road to Zero Emissions, More Jobs, More Income and No Pollution.* Sheffield, England: Greenleaf Publishing, 1998.

Pearson, David. *THE NATURAL HOUSE BOOK.* New York, NY: Simon & Schuster, Inc., Fireside Books, 1989.

St. John, Andrew, ed., *THE SOURCEBOOK FOR SUSTAINABLE DESIGN: A Guide to Environmentally Responsible Building Materials and Processes.* Boston, MA: Architects for Social Responsibility/Boston Society of Architects, 1992.

Starkman, Dean. "How Much Wood?" *THE WALL STREET JOURNAL,* Monday, September 27, 1999, front page.